Come Fly with Me

Tips for Traveling with Children
Anywhere in the World Effortlessly and Fearlessly

By

Lizabeth K Kohler

ISBN: 1482085135

ISBN 13: 9781482085136

Library of Congress Control Number: 2013901797
CreateSpace Independent Publishing Platform
North Charleston, South Carolina

To my three children, who I dragged all over the world
And to my husband and traveling companion

Why I Wrote This Book

I wish I had known how to make travel easier and more fun when I first started traveling with children. There are lots of books on places to visit, but not many on how to make travel with kids easy. Despite all the hassles, there is still nothing I would rather do than travel with my kids.

My husband, Mike, and I come from families that have always traveled extensively. My grandparents traveled to more than 120 countries. My parents rarely spend more than ten consecutive days at home and at any time might be found in Bhutan, Botswana, or Barbados. They are the only people I know who have actually been to both Timbuktu and Tasmania! Mike's mother grew up in Switzerland and as a travel agent has spent her life exploring the world. Our kids actually have four grandparents who have all been to Antarctica.

The first trip I took to Europe as an adult with kids was when my oldest son was three and my daughter was a year old. I have done it many times since, and I can tell you how to make traveling with children a lot easier.

I have been to forty-five of the fifty states, and my children have been to about half. They have also been to Switzerland, England, France, Kenya, Tanzania, Egypt, Rwanda, Peru, Costa Rica, Italy, Mexico, Greece, the Dominican Republic, Jamaica, Grand Cayman, and Quebec. I have visited an additional ten or so countries. I know what it is like to be a traveling kid and also a parent traveling with kids. I started early—I took my first international trip when I was three months old. Traveling has new conveniences (information at your fingertips) and difficulties (airport security), and with a few tips and checklists, it can be a whole lot easier. I hope that you'll learn just a few and be inspired to show your family the world.

I am also a very organized person who keeps many, many lists, several of which I share here. I have organized this book into sections. Feel free to skip around and go directly to the information you need. Topics covered include:

- Getting started
- Where in the world to go
- How to travel kids of all ages
- Planning and organizing a great trip
- Tips
- Websites, apps, and blogs
- Fun vacation ideas

Contents

Why Travel with Kids?

There is nothing better than traveling. There is so much to see, whether it is the Caribbean Sea's blue waters, the crumbling ancient ruins of Greece, the majestic castles of Europe, or offbeat places like the Corn Palace and Graceland in the United States. African lions, Bengal tigers, and grizzly bears will take you to Africa, India, and Canada. Whether you prefer awesome nature like the Grand Canyon, fabulous museums like the Louvre, or the physical thrill of a hike or a day of skiing, it is all so fascinating and interesting. Eating new cuisine, trying a different sport, shopping in a quirky toy store, and observing haute couture are all cultural experiences. Traveling is always great adventure.

A family vacation is an entirely different experience from traveling alone or with a spouse. It is a tremendous way for your family to bond and enjoy adventures together, some planned and others unplanned. There will be ups and downs, and whether you go near or far, it is always interesting and gets you away from your everyday routine. It opens your eyes to new ideas and sends you home regenerated. It is also one of the greatest gifts you can give your kids. You will look back and remember the wonderful trips and fun times you had together.

You can travel fifty or five thousand miles and have a great time. In the United States, you can visit Washington, DC, New York City, New Orleans, Chicago, Dallas, Las Vegas, San Francisco, or Portland and you will experience something new in each place. You can see our national parks, ballparks, or amusement parks. You will meet delightful people from all over the world. Visiting the Colosseum in Rome, Versailles outside Paris, the Great Wall in China, or the Acropolis in Greece brings history class to life for children. However, you don't even have to take them to the major sights for them to learn something new. You can have a gelato or talk to a taxi driver to experience a new culture. Travel makes the world less foreign and more understandable.

Traveling with children can seem overwhelming and daunting, but it doesn't have to be. Many people worry what their children will eat in France, how they will sit on a fifteen-hour flight to Australia, how they can possibly be entertained all the way to Europe. They worry what to do if the kids get sick in Mexico or what to do if they want to go to Europe and their kids don't like art museums. Don't worry. With a good plan and a good attitude, you can do it.

Part I
Getting Started

Some Things to Consider

There are so many fun and interesting places on this planet that one of the hardest decisions to make is where to go. There are five factors that, combined with a sensible itinerary, will help you plan the best vacation for you and your kids.

Start by considering:
- Your children's ages
- Your family's interests
- Your family temperament
- Your hassle tolerance
- Your budget

Your children's ages

A sensible itinerary taking the ages of your children into consideration is crucially important. There are ideal trips for families with infants, toddlers, elementary-age children, or teens. Depending on the children's ages, these may be beach or mountain vacations, cruises, driving trips, international destinations, or adventure trips. Many places are good for all ages, but it is important to recognize that some are geared for a particular age group. For instance, don't try to take a two-year-old hike up the Inca trail to Machu Picchu. Making the ages of your children a primary consideration when planning will make your travels both easier and more enjoyable.

A few questions to consider:

What can the youngest child do?

Walk

Hike

Ski

Swim

Sightsee

Do any children need naps?
Are you going to divide up so everyone can do what he or she wants?
Do you want to do everything together?
Will there be a babysitter?

When I was in the hotel room with the baby while the others were off on fun adventures I sometimes wished I had hired a babysitter. Other times I enjoyed the peace and quiet.

Your family's interests

What to see and do involves compromise on everyone's part, but think about what activities the children would like. Parents have to view this as a family trip, not an adult trip with the kids. You might have to go to tacky amusement parks in Paris, and the kids might have to put up with a dull museum or two. Have a plan that will interest everyone. Each activity does not have to excite everyone at all times, but make it a trip that overall everyone will enjoy.

Most people try to do too much. You don't want to be constantly on the go. Some energetic families or those with teens can do more. For most everyone, vacations are for fun, and nobody wants to spend more than two hours a day in a car. If you try to see all of Europe or all the national parks in one vacation, it is simply not going to be fun. One or two long travel days are OK if you are going for a week, but these should be the exception. Some kids are better at flying, others better at riding long distances in a car. Either way, do not spend so much time traveling that you can't enjoy the vacation.

If you try to see everything in Paris, it is better than trying to see all of France or all of Europe on one trip. Go see five national parks in ten days. Or spend a weekend seeing Los Angeles or New York. People will tell you that you can't go abroad for a week—you can if you stay put once you get there. Have a home base and venture out from there if possible. Do you like beaches, skiing, hiking, sightseeing, shopping, golf, museums, amusement parks zoos, or fine dining? You need a focus for the trip. You don't have to do this with every vacation, and, of course, you may do many different activities, but it is good to have a purpose to the trip.

Ask yourself, "What is the purpose of the trip?"
Play a sport
Experience a different culture
Go sightsee
Go on a true adventure
Relax
Other _____

If you want to show your teenage children Europe, then the focus might be sightseeing and museums. However, you will also go shopping and eat at restaurants. If you are more interested in physical fitness and sports, then a ski trip or hiking experience will be a better fit.

Make sure there is something for everyone to do that he or she will like. Sometimes your children are very different—say, the oldest likes physical activity, the middle child likes shopping, and the youngest likes visiting the zoo. You need to find a place where you can do all of those things. Now, the children will all need to compromise and do things they don't like sometimes, but *there has to be something on the vacation that everyone really likes.* You could do a theme-based trip, such as seeing ballparks, amusement parks, skateboard parks, or beaches. You could visit the top golf resorts, spas, gardens, sporting events, cities, museums, or highest peaks. You could visit the sights from a favorite movie like National Treasure or Night at the Museum. Let your imagination soar. See the last section of this book for ideas.

Your family's temperament

Consider whether your family likes to sit around a beach or pool and read and hang out. Or are you a family that is always on the go, doing things at all times? Would you like a lot of physical activity? Does making the most of your vacation time mean doing as many things as you possibly can? You might have some members who need more down time, while others may need to be doing something all the time. If so, both will have to compromise, so choose a trip that involves some of each. If you are an active family and want to see Europe, maybe a bike trip across France would be better than visiting museums. There are fabulous trips for everyone of every age, interest, and ability. You just have to find the trip that fits your family. Planning a vacation that will appeal to everyone in the family is the tricky part. Mom and Dad remain the decision makers, but they need to keep in mind the interests of everyone on the trip.

Your hassle tolerance

There are families with all different tolerances for hassles. Some are laid-back and go with the flow. Others are the worriers, and if things don't go right, it totally stresses them out. Then there are the moderates who are in between. This is different than energy level. This has to do with your tolerance for bumps in the road. When your flight gets cancelled, are you OK to take the next one out or does it send you into a real panic? What if your hotel is overbooked? Tickets are sold out or the museum is closed? If these send you into a panic or stress you out, then a vacation with three flight changes or other complicated logistics might not be your best option.

Your budget

Budget is obviously a factor. Staying at the Ritz in Paris requires a different budget than camping at a local campground. So, how much do you have to spend on this vacation? You might look at where the dollar is strong. Central and South America are usually relatively cheap, and Europe is often expensive. Many places can be done either cheaply or luxuriously. Others, such as adventure trips in Africa, are often hard to get to, so the flights are quite expensive even if the accommodations are cheap. Consider traveling off-season to avoid crowds and save a little money.

Fill out the worksheet in Appendix A to help you.

Where to Dream Up Travel Ideas

There are many sources for both practical information and inspiration on vacation destinations. Travel agents used to be the go-to resource for this, but now that they are fading, the best sources are the Internet, books, magazines, newspapers, and friends.

• Internet: Google places you might be interested in. There are also lots of blogs and top ten lists online—I have included some of these in the back of this book. There is so much information out there it is impossible for me to even make a dent in the list. If you have a particular interest and destination in mind, try Googling the destination, the word top, and your interest: for example, "Montreal top restaurants" or "Yellowstone top hiking trails." Facebook your friends for ideas. Search around and you will find a wealth of information. For travel deals or just inspiration, check out the websites for Groupon, Vacationist, and Jetsetter, for starters—many more are listed at the end of this book.

• Guidebooks: Read some guidebooks. My favorite is 1000 Places to See Before You Die by Patricia Schultz for snippets on a thousand destinations. The Travel Book by Lonely Planet is another favorite. National Geographic has several I would recommend, including The 10 Best of Everything, An Ultimate Guide for Travelers and 500 Journeys of a Lifetime.

• Magazines: The magazines I like are Conde Nast Traveler, National Geographic Traveler, Travel + Leisure, and Outside. There are ideas in parenting magazines and almost any lifestyle magazine as well. Newspapers almost always have a travel section.

Go to your local library for travel guides—you can get preliminary information on places you think might be interesting without having to buy a mountain of books. Browsing travel guides, you'll learn what there is to do in particular cities, regions, and countries that might be fun for your family. Fodor's and other guidebooks have specific recommendations on what to do with children, so once you narrow down your potential destinations you can take a look at those recommendations and see if they sound appealing to your family. I also keep a file in my desk and every time I read about an interesting place, I put the article in my file. Whenever I can't think of where I want to go next, I refer to my file for ideas.

To figure out where to go, ask yourself these important questions:

> What is the purpose of the vacation?
> What can the children do?
> What do we want to do?
> When do we want to go?
> What is our budget?

Once you have narrowed down the destination, you can learn more from a travel guide. There are many of these, but some of the more popular ones include:

Access Guides
Fodor's
Michelin for Europe
Time Out
Let's Go
Insight Guides
Insider's
DK Witness
WorldwideToursDirectory.com

For budget travel I would recommend:
Frommer's
Lonely Planet
Rough Guides
Moon Guidebooks

Some of these guides offer information online.

You can also check out online travel forums. Many of the guidebooks have forums. Check out Tripadvisor.com and VirtualTourist.com or Google the destination. Most places have a tourism office online with information about upcoming events as well as local attractions.

Part II

Where in the World to Go

Beach, Tennis, or Golf Resorts

Ages: All ages
Interests: Golf, tennis, relaxing, culture
Family Temperament: Energetic, mild-mannered, or calm
Hassle Factor: Low
Budget: $-$$$$

Ages:

A resort vacation is fun for kids and adults of any age. Everyone can find something interesting to do at a beach resort. For families with infants, this is the perfect place to start. Parents of infants are tired from getting up all night. Raising an infant can be physically and mentally exhausting—why make a vacation more work? You don't want to feel like you'll need a vacation from the vacation when it is over. Typically, a resort has a convenient setup for new parents, with the hotel close to the beach and pool, so that when the baby needs to nap, you can all just go in and take a break from the sun. You won't feel like you are missing anything.

Any age will be happy at the beach. Everyone likes a little sunshine in the middle of winter. Most kids love pools and beaches. There are often kids' camps, which are a fun way to meet other children and do some arts and crafts and games. There is tennis and golf for almost any level. When the kids get old enough, you can do those activities as a family. The only exception to this being the perfect vacation is with kids who cannot swim. This can be very stressful for the parents who have to watch every second. In this case, make sure one parent is on lifeguard duty and the pool is far from your accommodations.

My grandparents took my mom, her brother and sister, and all their families to a beach vacation every year for thirty years. It is an enjoyable vacation where all ages can find plenty to do.

Interests:

Resort vacations are among the easiest and most relaxing vacations a family can take. Imagine the beautiful, broad sandy beaches full of shells, children frolicking in the waves or by the pool. Most feature piña coladas, root beer, and wonderful Southern, Caribbean, or Mexican food. The only exertion is a few rounds of golf, a game of tennis, or a scenic bike ride. You can read by the pool, put the kids in camp, and sail, snorkel, or go for a spa treatment. The beach can be on an ocean or lake, so you can travel far or near to find one.

A resort vacation has something for almost every interest. If you like warm weather, reading, sitting by the sea, swimming for hours on end, or playing a set of tennis or round of golf, it's ideal. You can also stroll, bike, or collect seashells. Sometimes there is fabulous snorkeling, tremendous surfing, or fun sailing. It is warm and sunny and often tropical, and it is just a fun change of pace.

Family Temperament:

A resort vacation is also great for a variety of temperaments. Active people will find lots of sports to keep them occupied. The relaxers will find plenty of places to read a good book or sunbathe. There is usually some shopping and casual dining close by—not upscale or fabulous, but fun. It is a great family vacation that makes almost anyone happy. As the kids get older, you might combine the resort vacation with a little culture in the Caribbean, Africa, Asia, or Europe.

Hassle Factor:

This is a pretty hassle-free vacation. It is usually easy to get to, everyone is entertained, and there is not much to worry about. Even the most stressed parents can handle a resort vacation.

Budget:

Resort vacations can fit any budget, as they can range from a super-luxury vacation at the Four Seasons in Nevis to a beach at a nearby lake. Another option to consider is traveling off-season. Hawaii, the Caribbean, and Mexico are pretty much the same temperature year-round, so you might try them in summer and they will be much less expensive. However, be sure to check for hurricane or rainy seasons in the region you're considering. You can almost always find a beach resort within a relatively short distance from your home, so getting there is usually easy. You can also go somewhere more exotic and fancy. There is a resort for every budget.

Accommodations:

For most families, it is best if you can find a resort where everything is together—tennis, golf, beach, etc. You can walk everywhere and it is all very convenient. If you have more than one child or any children over the age of three, a condo can be the best option. With a condo, you don't have to go out for every meal and can eat a quick breakfast at home or make basic sandwiches that everyone likes. A few dinners out are usually enough. Older kids can dine out more, but even they probably prefer to eat pizza at home with a good movie occasionally. Mom and Dad should go out by themselves at least once, if you can hire a resort babysitter or bring someone with you. I also like condos since I am fair-skinned and I can get my kids out of the sun for a few hours in the heat of the day to prevent sunburn. A condo with a living room is much more comfortable for board games, reading, and relaxing than a hotel room—avoiding midday sun can be an opportunity for family time.

Tips and Suggestions:

There are too many resorts to list—there are wonderful ones in the United States, Africa, Asia, Australia, and Europe. Remember that beaches in the United States and the Caribbean are usually nice and sandy, but many in Europe, South America, and Central America are rocky. Make sure you know what you are getting. Rocky beaches are fascinating, but not great for little kids trying to build a sandcastle or playing in the waves. There are many websites and books dedicated to where to go for an excellent beach vacation. I have a few suggestions, but do some research. Be careful to avoid super-crowded all-inclusives or prices that seem too good to be true. It won't be fun if you can't get a spot on the beach or a chair by the pool. As the kids get older, consider a resort in a location where you can experience a little culture, see a new city nearby, or visit a national park.

Beach Destinations:

Long Island
New Jersey
Cape Cod
South Carolina
Florida—both coasts
California
Hawaii
Jamaica
Barbados
Puerto Rico
Virgin Gorda

Rocky but interesting beaches can be found in
Italy
Greece
France
Spain
Portugal
Mexico

Tops for Tennis:

Rancho Valencia, California
Wild Dunes, South Carolina
The Broadmoor, Colorado
Ponte Vedra, Florida
Palmetto Dunes, South Carolina
Kiawah, South Carolina
Sea Pines, South Carolina
The Boulders, Arizona
Colony Beach and Tennis, Florida
Mauna Kea, Hawaii
La Jolla, California

Tops for Family Golf:

The Boulders, Colorado
Sea Island, Georgia
Greenbriar, West Virginia
Kiawah, South Carolina
Amelia Island, Florida
Pinehurst, North Carolina
Pebble Beach, California
Troon North, Arizona
Manele Bay, Hawaii
Las Vegas Resort, Nevada
Snowmass, Colorado

Mountains

Mountain vacations in winter or summer are vastly different experiences, but equally wonderful.

• Winter: A mountain destination is a photographer's dream. Snow-capped mountains are simply gorgeous, and pines are picturesque bent over with the weight of a fresh snowfall. Around the winter holidays, quaint mountain towns dress up in lights for the holidays, which can really fill you with the festive spirit. You can often go on a sleigh ride or maybe see Santa.

• Spring: Spring skiing is awesome. You can enjoy some warm sunshine amidst the snowflakes. Often you eat outside on the top of the mountain or enjoy a drink after a day of skiing at the bottom of the mountain. It is definitely warmer. (Watch for sunburn!)

• Summer: Mountains in the summer are just as magnificent as in winter or spring, if not more so. The very tops of the mountains might still have a dusting of snow, the skies are blue and beautiful, and the wildflowers span an entire spectrum of colors. The lakes are full of trout, and the fresh mountain air can make for a peaceful and wonderful family vacation. Mountain destinations designed for skiing in winter are often perfect in summer for hiking, biking, whitewater rafting, or horseback riding. You might even see a moose, bear, or hawk.

Skiing

Ages: 4 and up
Interests: Outdoors, winter sports, photography, family togetherness
Family Temperament: Outgoing, adventurous, athletic, curious, easygoing, energetic
Hassle Factor: High
Budget: $$$-$$$$ (unless you live near a ski resort)

Ages:

A ski vacation is ideal for children four and older because that's when kids really learn to ski. Kids have to be potty-trained to go to ski school; however, almost all resorts have day care for younger kids. In Switzerland and probably other parts of Europe, kids learn to ski as soon as they learn to walk and have instruction in the morning and racing in the afternoon. No wonder they're such good skiers! Now, if most of your kids can ski but you also have a younger child, don't let that stop you from enjoying a great ski vacation. The younger child can stay with a babysitter or go to day care.

We went to Switzerland with my in-laws when my oldest was four. It was his first time on skis, but since kids in Switzerland learn to ski as soon as they can walk he was the oldest and largest kid in the class. There is no such thing as half-day ski school. He started with instruction in the morning, followed by racing in the afternoon. American ski resorts are a little more laid-back, but won't let a child in ski school until he or she is potty-trained.

Interests:

Whether you prefer skiing, snowboarding, snowshoeing, sledding, photography, dining, or shopping, you can find great enjoyment in a ski vacation. It is among the most picturesque of vacations. Skiing can be enjoyed by skiers of any ability, and nonskiers will find plenty to do as well. Skiing is a great life-long sport that is much easier to learn at a young age.

You can also just sit by the fire in the lodge and read a good book, play games, and enjoy the mountain views from indoors. There are also hot tubs, swimming pools, spas, and shopping for those who have more relaxation in mind. The restaurants are usually lots of fun and casual. Even the fine-dining choices at ski resorts rarely require much more than ski clothes. There really are options for everyone, nonskier and avid skier alike.

A ski vacation is different from a beach vacation in that family members go their separate ways during the day and then come together in the afternoon. The kids often go to ski school all day while Mom and Dad ski either together or separately, depending on their abilities. Because everyone basically does his or her own thing all day and then the family regroups after ski school, this type of vacation does not always provide as much togetherness as other sorts of vacations. This can be a good thing in that it gives family members a break and allows them time to do as they please. Kids are also tired at night and tend to sleep really well, and you feel like everyone got fresh air and exercise. As the kids get better and can ski on their own, they will ski with one parent or the whole family, and this is lots of fun too.

Family Temperament:

For an active family, a ski vacation is fabulous. Everyone gets lots of exercise, fresh air, and wonderful mountain food and is usually exhausted by the end of the day. However, if they are not tired after a day of skiing, there is tubing and ice skating at night. The restaurants are often festive and casual, with families in mind, offering great atmosphere that kids love. The kids learn to ski and improve so quickly they are sure to pass up the adults in no time. The mountain air is exhilarating and the scenery is beautiful. Most resorts also offer little boutiques with mountain supplies, clothing, and fudge for fun shopping. So this vacation is definitely geared for the more active family.

Hassle Factor:

For families with young children, this can be a stressful vacation that involves a lot of organization, patience, and time. It requires waking up early to get everyone in four layers of clothing, ski boots, helmets, gloves, and goggles. Ski boots are hard to walk in, so getting around will take time. Then you will need to register them for ski school and rent skis. These systems are not the most efficient, so you will need to get there before the lessons begin at 8:30 a.m. However, it gets much easier as the kids get older and can carry their own skis and graduate from ski school. Also if you stay near the ski school it really helps a lot.

Budget:

This can be a rather expensive vacation. First, it depends on where you live and where you need to go. If you need to fly to your destination, you will have to figure in your flight expenses. There are expensive resorts like Vail and Aspen, and then there are cheaper resorts like Steamboat, where kids under twelve ski free, and smaller, more regional resorts. Where you stay will affect the prices of lift tickets and accommodations. You might need to figure in the cost of ski school, ski rentals, and a car. Meals can get expensive too. This is not a cheap vacation in most instances unless you have friends or relatives with free accommodations nearby.

Accommodations:

This is one vacation where I would definitely recommend staying in a condo rather than a hotel, if possible. You'll need space for a lot of overstuffed luggage, layers and layers of clothes, and everybody's equipment—so the bigger the accommodations, the better. I would also try to stay as close to the ski school as possible. Just because a condo is marketed as ski-in/ski-out doesn't mean a five-year-old can ski in or out on that run. The run near your room could be a black diamond run which is too difficult for most kids. You do not want to have to drive or carry skis too far. Since skis are very heavy and ski school starts fairly early, it is a lot easier if you are located close to the school. It is also unbelievable how long it can take to get kids ready with all the layers of clothes, boots, helmets, mittens, and so forth.

The final reason to get a condo is that a ski vacation is physically tiring, and it is easier to feed kids in a condo than take them out after a full day of skiing. You might want to go out for a few meals, but it is nice to have the option of eating at the condo. Breakfast is also easier if you can grab a quick bite at the condo before ski school. A washer and dryer also come in handy—gloves and snow pants get very wet and need to dry before the next day.

Tips and Suggestions:

Ski school

Ski school is fun for the kids and a great way to make friends. It is also the most economical way to teach your kids to ski. The school provides skis, instruction, and lunch for about $100 per day. Most ski schools have a "magic carpet," which is basically a conveyor belt to take the little kids up the hill so they don't have to side step or use a tow rope to get back up the hill. There are fun little kiddie parks with wood cutouts shaped like bears or snowmen or other fun things to ski around. The instructors know how to teach kids to ski in a pizza shape (snowplow) or french fries (parallel). There are terrain parks with jumps for the older kids. Overall, ski schools make learning to ski fun. The instructors are often young and energetic, with lots of enthusiasm, and the kids think they are cool. The instructors also take the kids to the best and least crowded parts of the mountain. At the end of each day, the instructors tell the kids what to work on and what they've achieved to motivate them to move to the next level. Over the course of a week, kids can go from a nonskier to a solid blue-run skier or better. Overall, ski school is the best option for most kids and families.

However, some kids hate ski school. They usually don't like it if there are too many kids in the class and they have to wait to go down the mountain. The other reason children might not like ski school is if they are shy and don't like to be left with a lot of strangers for the day. In either case, you have two choices: either the children will end up skiing with you or you will have to hire a private instructor. Skiing with you might involve some tears because most likely you are not a trained instructor and don't know how to teach children to ski. Also, you are their parent, and so when they are frustrated in learning this sport they will not be shy about letting you know. The best way for children to learn to ski is from someone other than their parents, otherwise it can cause too many fights when you are trying to take a nice family vacation. Furthermore, if you are a proficient skier yourself, you will not be able to ski the black runs you had envisioned if you share all of your time on the slopes with your kids.

The alternative option is to hire a private ski instructor. This is extremely expensive (approximately $700 per day), but if this is not an issue, your child will learn to ski very quickly. It might be worth it if it is a busy time of year and there will be twelve kids in the ski-school class or if you have a shy or fussy child. You can also do a half day of private instruction and/or have several of your children share the lesson with the same instructor.

Babysitting

A ski vacation is not an ideal trip for a napping infant, but it can be done. If you are bringing a baby, there are several options to avoid sitting in the condo all day. You can hire a babysitter, bring one from home, or use day care. It depends how much skiing you want to do, what your budget is, and how fussy your child is with strangers. Resort babysitters usually are quite expensive ($30/hour), but they are good and will give your baby whatever they need. They will walk them, feed them, play games, and give them a nap. Now, you never know what you are going to get. You might get Nanny McPhee, Mary Poppins, or some young ski bum. Most are very qualified, but personalities will run the gamut.

Alternatively, ski resorts also have day care for a very reasonable price. If you don't have a fussy baby who needs to nap, that might be a good option. If the child is social, he or she might even prefer that. Another option, if you have the space, is to bring a babysitter from home. That is good in that the child would be familiar with the babysitter. If you are paying the nanny a weekly salary anyway and just have to buy a plane ticket, you might come out even compared with hiring a resort babysitter—it depends on how many hours you need and the price of the plane ticket. Determine your comfort level with day care and a new babysitter. Then determine your budget and you will make the right choice.

How to pick a ski resort

So what part of the world do you want to ski? The skiing in the western United States is great and tends to be less icy than the East

Coast, but many of the best skiers come from the East. If you live in the East, you know that there are many wonderful resorts there as well.

Skiing in Europe and South America can offer different cultural experiences. Skiing is part of the culture in Switzerland, France, and elsewhere, and a ski vacation in these countries also offers a glimpse into their cuisine and customs. European skiing is usually above the tree line, and sometimes the snow is a little more unpredictable.

US Ski Resorts:

For families of every level: Vail, Snowmass, Steamboat, Whistler

For pampering: Deer Valley, Telluride, Aspen

For experts: Snowbird, Taos, Jackson Hole

With great shopping: Vail, Aspen, Sun Valley, Jackson Hole

Others to consider: Park City, Breckenridge, Keystone, Lake Tahoe

There is also skiing in South America, Asia, and other more exotic places—there are options all over the world. For a less ambitious vacation, there are even options in Wisconsin and Ohio. Once you get your region figured out, you will need to consider the level of difficulty. Some resorts are primarily for experts, while others are very family-oriented with easier terrain. If Mom or Dad wants more of a challenge, then you need a mountain village that has everything, like Vail or Whistler. If you want a luxurious, easy resort, then go someplace like Deer Valley or Snowmass. If you have older kids and you are all experts, you might try someplace like Taos or Snowbird. There are many to choose from in every category.

Next, consider how far away from the airport you want to be. The closer to the airport, the more crowded the resort will be—so you have to weigh your options. If you are going during a holiday, it would be better to drive a little further to avoid crowds and long lift lines. If you are going for a long weekend during a nonpeak time, go for convenience. Finally, when looking for a ski resort, you should also consider what else you want. Restaurants and nightlife, good shopping, skating, or tubing? Do you want a town close by or a resort vacation? Consider your budget because ski resorts and accommodations vary widely. A ski vacation is not cheap in comparison to most others, but there are condos and hotels of every price under the sun.

Equipment

You can rent or buy skis, boots, and poles. Most people on vacation will rent. It really is a hassle to be traveling with children and ski equipment. I think it only makes sense to own if you are skiing more than three or four weeks a year.

Premium skis and boots cost only $50/day to rent. Good skis are several thousand dollars after you get bindings put on and purchase boots. Also, the technology of skis changes year to year, and you can get the latest and greatest if you rent. And remember that kids' rentals usually come with the purchase of ski school.

The downside to renting is that it takes time to be fitted. You have to allow an hour for this, so try to do it the evening before you plan to ski or once you get the kids into ski school. If you feel this would be better done at home, you could rent at home and ship the skis to your resort so you can start skiing as soon as you arrive and not worry about long lines. However, then you need to figure out how to get the skis home.

I wouldn't recommend buying skis for vacation unless you are unusually picky. You will have to deal with the risk of airlines losing skis, the hassle of shipping skis, transporting skis in ski racks, etc. If you live near a ski resort and are skiing more than three weeks a year, you are not vacation skiing—go ahead, buy your skis.

Summer in the Mountains

Ages: Any
Interests: Outdoors, hiking, biking, rafting, fishing, photography
Family Temperament: Any
Hassle Factor: Low
Budget: $-$$$

Mountain vacations are not just fun in the winter. There is no place prettier than the mountains in summer, with wildflowers in bloom and snow-peaked summits. There are also so many activities that you cannot do at home, at least in the suburbs of Chicago where I live. Most resorts offer hiking, whitewater rafting, horseback riding, and much more. They often have kids' camps, giant slides, mountain biking, and fishing.

The ski resorts out west have a real Western flair; you can go on a trail ride for a pancake breakfast, watch a rodeo, and enjoy a steak dinner. They always have golf and tennis as well. The East Coast ski resorts—in Vermont, New Hampshire, and upstate New York—are equally pretty, with more of a quaint New England flavor. Some are on lakes with swimming and boating, which is fun even if it is a tad chilly.

Ages:

Any age can enjoy a week in the mountains in summertime. It just depends on what activities you choose to do. If you're bringing a baby, there are backpack carriers for infants so they can hike with you. There are long and short hikes. Some resorts have pools, so you can just sit by the water. Little kids can go to camps, fish, hike, and go to the playground. Bigger kids might like horseback riding or whitewater rafting, as well as an all-day hike.

Interests:

This trip is geared for families with an interest in the outdoors. You do not have to be proficient at anything, just have an enthusiasm for the outdoors. You can sit and read while looking at the mountains or be more active and go hiking, biking, horseback riding, or fishing. There is beautiful scenery perfect for photography. The food is great and a mountain vacation is a wonderful way to escape to the outdoors.

We went to Vail in the summer and there were skateboard competitions and BMX bike demonstrations. My kids really enjoyed it since they don't have much of that in Chicago.

Family Temperament:

This trip is geared for almost any temperament. If you are an active family or more of the relaxing type, there is plenty to do. Most resorts have spas and pools as well as kids' camps and a myriad of activities for the active family.

Hassle Factor:

This is a low-hassle trip. All you have to do is get there. The rest is up to you, and you can just go day by day. Not much organization is involved unless you want some structured fishing or whitewater rafting trips. This type of vacation can be as low-key or action-packed as you desire. Even the action-packed option is easy to organize and reservations for the activities only need to be made a week in advance. If you do want to go fly-fishing, whitewater rafting, or horseback riding, call ahead to make your reservations.

Budget:

This vacation can be as cheap or as expensive as you desire. You might have to factor in flights, but the accommodations could be a tent, the Four Seasons, or anything in between. However, the rates at most mountain-area hotels in the summer are about half of what they are during ski season. It is considered off-season.

Accommodations:

At this time of year, location is not as important. You can stay in a little lodge or a five-star hotel. It depends on what you want and your budget. I like being relatively close to restaurants, hiking trails, and town. However, you don't have to be right next door. This should be a leisurely vacation, so if you have a fifteen-minute drive, it's OK. If you have young children, I again would make sure I had a condo, if possible, so as not to have to go out for every meal. I also like having the living room so I can spread out and relax.

Tips and Suggestions:

There are lots of wonderful mountain resorts both on the West and East Coasts as well as all over Europe. A few of my picks are:
Vail, Colorado
Aspen, Colorado

Sun Valley, Idaho
Breckenridge, Colorado
Telluride, Colorado
Deer Valley, Utah
Whistler, Canada
Lake Louise, Canada
Taos, New Mexico
Stowe, Vermont
Jackson Hole, Wyoming
St. Moritz, Switzerland
Zermatt, Switzerland
Megeve, France

Cruises

Ages: 5 and up
Interests: Learning about a different culture, pools, entertainment
Family Temperament: Patient, relaxed, or active
Hassle Factor: Low-medium
Budget: $-$$$

Ages:

Cruises are great for almost any age group, depending on where you are going. However, I never felt comfortable on a boat trip until my kids could swim pretty well. The other reason I suggest age five and up is so children can go on the excursions, which tend to be geared for that age group. Now, if you are cruising to the Caribbean and will just be going to a beach and pool, I don't think your children need to be five.

I also think cruises appeal to any age group because they offer so much, for everyone and every interest: lectures, exercise classes, movies, shows at night, casinos for adults, swimming pools, miniature golf, kids' clubs, teen night, and, on some cruises, skating rinks, rock climbing, and more. I will make suggestions on which cruise lines to choose, but there are plenty that offer entertainment and fun excursions off the boat for every age group. It really is a trip where everyone from five to 105 can have a great time.

Interests:

Cruises go to a variety of locations—pretty much anywhere there is water. Alaska, Europe, South America, Asia, Australia, the Caribbean, Mexico, and parts of North America are popular destinations. There are probably a hundred different excursions in each location. Some are active, like whitewater rafting, while others are more nature-oriented, like whale watching. And then there are train trips and walks around town. There really is something for absolutely every interest. Depending on the location, there will be beaches, golf, museums, snorkeling, fishing, rafting, castles, cooking classes, monuments, and more. Most have innovative side trips that you would never think of. In Alaska, for example, our cruise offered whale watching, whitewater rafting to a glacier, fishing for crabs, and riding on a sled driven by huskies. You can also arrange your own excursions.

Family Temperament:

This vacation is best for families with patience because there are a lot of people on a cruise. You all have to get on and off together and eat together, so while it is as organized as possible, there will be some waiting in line. A cruise can be for an active family or one that likes to relax because there really is something for everyone to do.

Hassle Factor:

For families, a major advantage of a cruise vacation is you are not driving from place to place with kids. You can see Europe and not have to change hotels every night. You can drag the kids to a museum, castle, or significant sight, and then they can go back to the boat and play basketball. You can see parts of the world you wouldn't be able to see except from a boat, such as the coast of Alaska. However, the best thing is that everything is organized for you: rooms, meals, activities, entertainment, etc. You just sign up and the cruise does the rest.

Budget:

There are cruises for every budget. Cruises themselves are not very expensive and can be a cheap way to travel. The excursions and drinks or special restaurants are the expensive part. If you are on a budget, just do some of the cheaper excursions. For example, in Alaska we skipped the helicopter rides and trips with the huskies because they were more than I wanted to spend, but we found other trips that were more in our budget. Some cruise lines to look at are Disney, Royal Caribbean, Princess, Norwegian, Cunard, Celebrity, and, at the top of the line, Crystal. There are many more as well, but this list should get you started.

Accommodations:

Royal Caribbean and Disney seem to be the most kid-friendly, but more and more boats are adding kids' programs. Princess and Holland are also pretty kid-friendly. Check out CruiseCritic.com for more information.

The rooms on cruise ships are small, but you don't spend that much time in your room, so the size doesn't really matter.

Tips and Suggestions:

Make sure the cruise line and location are not of the booze-cruise variety. The longer trips and more exotic locations will not be. The three-day cruise in the Caribbean might be more of a drinking crowd than the twelve days in Europe. Also, if you go on the Disney cruise, you are going to get primarily families.

Book early for the best choice of rooms. You will need to book ahead so that you can get two rooms close to each other. If you have three children, booking rooms together can be even trickier. Some cruise lines don't have rooms for three, and if you are looking for a double near a triple you will need to book well in advance.

Also, book your excursions early, because those sell out. Alternatively, you can do excursions separately from the cruise line. For example, you could get a tour guide in Europe or go snorkeling in the Caribbean with another company.

We took a cruise in Alaska and the kids loved it. It was such an easy vacation. The kids enjoyed fishing for crabs, watching the jumping whales, hearing the glaciers crack, whitewater rafting in wetsuits, and seeing the huskies. They also liked the kids' programs on board—I realize that not all kids do, but ours played basketball and miniature golf, watched movies, and went rock climbing. We swam every day in the pool, even though the air in Alaska was a bit cold. The food was not spectacular, but fine, and Royal Caribbean also offered alternative restaurants that were quite good.

National Parks

Ages: 1 and up
Interests: Outdoors, hiking, horseback riding, whitewater rafting, fishing, and photography
Family Temperament: Any
Hassle Factor: Low
Budget: $-$$

There are over fifty national parks in the United States. Teddy Roosevelt fought to preserve the national parks. He thought these areas were so special and beautiful that all Americans should have a chance to see them and that they should be preserved. I think he was right.

Age:

This trip is perfect for any child once he or she can walk because the main activity is hiking. Infants will also be OK, as long as you are OK with carrying them on your back. The parks are not really set up with babysitters the way a resort is. For three-year-olds to eighty-year-olds, it is a wonderful vacation. National parks are great for kids because they can run around, be noisy, do whatever they want. You can enjoy the beautiful scenery, get some exercise, and take some gorgeous photos. The parks are a fabulous place to take kids.

Interests:

National parks are geared for people who enjoy the outdoors. You do not have to be super-athletic or anything, but the main activities are hiking, horseback riding, whitewater rafting, and fishing. The parks offer very strenuous all-day or multi-day hikes to thirty-minute hikes geared for every level. You can also just go on a short walk and take pictures, have a picnic, and enjoy the scenery. There are usually kids' guides for nature walks. The national parks are among the most spectacular settings in the world.

In addition to seeing the parks, getting there is an active part of the vacation. Your family will see things that can only be seen if you drive across America You will see Wall Drug in South Dakota, Monument Valley in Utah and Graceland in Tennessee—places and experiences that would be missed from the air. You will see real cowboys and Native Americans and people from every socioeconomic background. It is a real eye-opener for kids and a good learning experience.

Family Temperament:

Any family temperament works here, from the energetic to the relaxed. You can do as much or as little activity as you want. You can just relax and sit by the campfire, have a picnic, and read. Or you can go mountain climbing, hiking, and horseback riding. It is all up to you.

Hassle Factor:

There is very little hassle involved here. You don't have to organize much or bring much. You wake up each morning and decide what to do that day. Now, I am going to warn you, if you decide to go to one of the most popular parks in the peak season, there will be too many people and it will be a hassle. The most popular parks are Yosemite, the Grand Canyon, and Yellowstone. My advice is to visit these in the off-season, September to May.

Budget:

National parks are the best value around. The parks cost about $10 per car and that's about the best deal anywhere. You cannot get into a movie for that price.

Accommodations:

For some reason, people think you need to camp out to see the national parks. This is definitely not true. The accommodations are not five-star. However, there are some nice lodges and they are a lot of fun. The lodges are old with lots of character. The hotels have a rustic feel, but perfect for kids. They serve good old American food, the prices are right, and there is a lot to do and see. The Best Westerns, another option have swimming pools, gift shops, and are clean and nice. There are lots of other hotels and motels as well. There just are not many fancy hotels.

Tips and Suggestions:

There are national parks, national monuments, and historical parks and monuments. There are also state parks and monuments. For the full list and further details, check out www.nps.gov. The most significant are the national parks. They are all very different and really indescribable. The most famous are the Grand Canyon, Yellowstone, and Yosemite. The others are equally spectacular and less crowded.

Crowds can be an issue in national parks, so it is best to go in the off-season if at all possible. Holidays such as Memorial Day, Fourth of July, and Labor Day will be especially crowded. Some national parks are closed in the winter and others in the summer—like Death Valley, due to the desert heat—so it is necessary to consult the national parks website and guidebooks to double-check when the parks are open.

Below is a list of all fifty-eight national parks. For some inspiration, Google any one of them and click on "images"—you will immediately see why they are such special places to visit.

ALASKA
Denali
Gates of the Arctic'
Glacier Bay
Katmai
Kenai Fjords
Kobuk Valley
Lake Clark
Wrangell-St. Elias

AMERICAN SAMOA
American Samoa

ARIZONA
Grand Canyon
Petrified Forest
Saguaro

ARKANSAS
Hot Springs

CALIFORNIA
Channel Islands
Death Valley
Joshua Tree
Kings Canyon
Lassen Volcanic
Redwood
Sequoia
Yosemite

COLORADO
Black Canyon of the Gunnison
Great Sand Dunes
Mesa Verde
Rocky Mountain

FLORIDA
Biscayne
Dry Tortugas
Everglades

HAWAII
Haleakala
Hawaii Volcanoes

IDAHO
Yellowstone
KENTUCKY
Mammoth cave

MAINE
Acadia

MICHIGAN
Isle Royale

MINNESOTA
Voyageurs

MONTANA
Glacier
Yellowstone

NEVADA
Great Basin

NEW MEXICO
Carlsbad Caverns

NORTH CAROLINA
Great Smoky Mountains

NORTH DAKOTA
Theodore Roosevelt

OHIO
Cuyahoga Valley

OREGON
Crater Lake

SOUTH CAROLINA
Congaree

SOUTH DAKOTA
Badlands
Wind Cave

TENNESSEE
Great Smoky Mountains

TEXAS
Big Bend
Guadalupe Mountains

US VIRGIN ISLANDS
Virgin Islands

UTAH
Arches
Bryce Canyon
Capitol Reef
Canyonlands
Zion

VIRGINIA
Shenandoah

WASHINGTON
Mount Ranier
North Cascades
Olympic

WYOMING
Grand Teton
Yellowstone

When I was young, my family took a five-week driving trip to see the national parks. Today, few people have that much time, so I have taken my kids on several different trips to see the parks. One good itinerary was nine days, starting and ending in Las Vegas. We saw the Grand Canyon, Arches, Canyonlands, Bryce, and Zion. Those are some of the best national parks with not much driving in between.

Cities

Ages: 4 and up
Interests: Culture, museums, zoos, aquariums, art, dining, parks, shopping
Family Temperament: Mildly to moderately active
Hassle Factor: Medium
Budget: $$-$$$$

Age:

This vacation is best for kids over four years old. Unless you have an extremely calm child, most children under four are not great in museums. There are things to do in most cities for almost any age child. The zoos, parks, and aquariums will be great for young children. Once kids turn about eight they will start to enjoy museums, but not for hours on end. Take them to an art museum for thirty minutes to an hour. Also use their interests as your guide. There are so many types of museums, from art to science to planetariums to nature. Many cities also offer children's museums. Older kids may complain, but they can visit any kind of museum and for a longer period of time. Remember that children really have not studied art or European history until high school, so the *Mona Lisa* may not be as interesting to them as the Coliseum.

Don't be silly like we were and try to take a one-year-old to New York City. We had a very energetic first child and the last place he belonged was a museum. The second worst place to take him was a restaurant. Consider your child's temperament!

Interests:

Cities are great for a wide array of interests. Most cities have an intriguing history and architecture, so if you are interested in either of those, there is plenty to do. They also usually have zoos, aquariums, and nature museums for people interested in animals and nature. For the art aficionados, there are plenty of art museums, from modern to Asian to Impressionist. The food lovers will find new and interesting restaurants and markets to try. When you need to burn off a little steam, there are great city parks, walking tours, and paths. When you are tired of culture, and especially if you have teenage girls, you can always go shopping. There are great and interesting shopping experiences all over the world.

Family Temperament:

Cities are really great for almost anyone, but they can be exhausting. There is a lot of walking and visual stimulation. If you are looking to sit around and relax, this is not the perfect vacation. Also, if you are looking to exercise and play sports, this is not ideal either. However, for middle-of-the-road families, it is perfect. There is enough to keep everyone interested and tons to do.

Hassle Factor:

This is not a hassle-free vacation because some kids will complain. They don't always want to go see museums, even if it is good for them. The key here is to mix museums with zoos and parks. Find kid-friendly things to do. There is also a lot of walking and going from one place to the next, which can be tiring. Just try not to do too much and be sure to schedule some down time.

Budget:

Most cities are fairly expensive. Even the cheapest hotels in New York City can run you several hundred dollars. The restaurants are expensive, and in most cases you will need to fly to get to the city. On top of that, you have taxis and museum admission tickets. Don't forget to figure in the shopping budget as well.

Accommodations:

You are going to have a hard time finding large accommodations. This is the one vacation where you will probably end up with several hotel rooms. Find a hotel that is close to the main attractions so you won't end up having to take expensive taxis everywhere. Kids like fun hotels, so whether your kids would like a fancy hotel or a modern one you should be able to find something for every taste. I usually try to find one with a pool so the children can burn off some steam and relax at the end of the day.

Tips and Suggestions:

Don't try to do too much in one day.
City vacations are best for three or four days.
Mix museums with kid-oriented outings.
Schedule down time.
Don't worry if you don't see all the tourist attractions.

Top Cities:

New York
Chicago
San Francisco
Boston
Atlanta
Washington, DC
Rome
Paris
Barcelona
Venice
London
Athens
Hong Kong

Disney World and Orlando

Ages: 4 and up
Interests: Disney, rides, entertainment, pools
Family Temperament: Moderate to active
Hassle Factor: Medium
Budget: $$$-$$$$

Disney is paradise for some and a nightmare for others. I happen to really like Disney World every now and then. It can be crowded, and there can be too much going on for little kids. However, depending on what your family likes to do, it can really be fun.

Ages:

People seem to think that Disney is for two-year-olds, when it really isn't. It is sensory overload, too expensive, and too much walking for very small children. Kids over four are fine for the experience. Even teenagers still have fun at Disney World. There are also great restaurants and bars in an area called Pleasure Island (think *Pinocchio*), so it is fun for adults too.

Interests:

Disney World, in Orlando, Florida, is comprised of Magic Kingdom, Epcot, MGM Studios, and Animal Kingdom. Close by you also have Sea World and Universal Studios, as well as water parks. So you really have to like rides, waterslides, and the movies.

Family Temperament:

If you are looking for a relaxing vacation, this might not be the best choice for you. However, for fun and entertainment, it is hard to beat. You have to be willing to walk with crowds and wait in lines. You also have to be a family where most everyone likes rollercoasters or amusement park rides. I have two kids who do not really like rides, so I think my husband and I actually enjoy Disney World more than our children. Meeting the characters can be fun, but some kids find it terrifying. This is for a moderately active family.

Hassle Factor:

This vacation has a moderate hassle factor. There are lines and crowds, but the hotels are conveniently located and Orlando is relatively easy to get to. Stay at one of the hotels on the monorail to make it less of a hassle. You will get into the park earlier and be able to leave midday, when the park is most crowded, to take a rest or swim, and then you can return when the crowds die down. There are books on how to do Disney World and I would read up on that before going. You can get Fast Passes which allow you to cut the lines and there are probably strategies on avoiding crowds and which rides to do first.

Budget:

This is a fairly expensive vacation; tickets cost around $50 per person per day. The hotels are not cheap, and you also need to figure in flights and food. Everything is pretty costly. You can go for just a few days rather than a week, both for your sanity and your budget.

Also, remember that you don't need to do all of Disney and the surrounding parks in one trip. Three days is the most I would recommend for a vacation here; do two or three parks and return for the rest another time. This will have you coming back for more rather than getting sick of it.

• Magic Kingdom: Magic Kingdom is geared for all ages and is what you think of when you think of Disney World. It has rides and characters, fireworks at night, and character breakfasts if your kids like to see the characters walking around. Be forewarned, many kids are frightened of the characters. Mickey and Minnie are really big.

• MGM Studios: MGM Studios shows how movies are made. It is sort of the Disney version of Universal Studios. Kids need to be six or older to really understand this and have fun here. There are exhibits showing how *Honey, I Shrunk the Kids* and *A Bug's Life* were made.

• Epcot: Epcot is great for adults and older kids. It is my favorite. It shows the culture of different countries and is pretty realistic, highlighting the food, dress, music, art and monuments from each region. After a visit, you will feel that you have traveled the world, and you and your family may leave with ideas for some future travel destinations. My favorites include the Beatles-like singers in England, the pagoda in China, and the Italian food. It is interesting, but little kids might not quite appreciate it.

• Animal Kingdom: Animal Kingdom is really fun. There are more animals than you will see on a trip to Africa. It is well done and there are also a few rides. You will see zebras, lions, elephants, and more. For the animal lover, it is a great experience. Again, not for toddlers who might be scared, but for anyone who likes animals.

Universal Studios and Sea World: These are fun too. Universal would appeal to older kids, probably over eight years old, who want to see how movies are made. Sea World is great, and their dolphin show is fun. They also have water rides and you can learn about sea creatures. Almost any age kid would love this.

There are also many water parks in the area that can be fun too, with wave pools, waterslides, and more.

Accommodations:

There are too many to even begin to tell you the pros and cons, but while the hotels on the monorail are more expensive, they are much easier to get to and from. They also offer special entry perks. However, there are plenty of other hotel options, and they will definitely be cheaper. There is a hotel for every theme, and if you are traveling with slightly older kids, I think these hotels off the monorail will be fine. There are buses shuttling you to the parks from these hotels.

I think I have stayed at the Polynesian more than any other hotel in the world. It is fun at any age. It's not fancy or anything, but a good middle-of-the-road hotel.

Tips and Suggestions:

Buy a guidebook for the whole scoop on Disney World. However, I would recommend staying three or four days at the most. A whole week is too much for me. My favorites are Magic Kingdom, Epcot, and Animal Kingdom. It is also really fun to go with extended family because every age loves Disney World.

Europe

Ages: 7 and up
Interests: Culture, history, museums, architecture, cuisine, outdoors, sports
Family Temperament: Calm to active
Hassle Factor: Medium
Budget: $$$$-$$$$$

Ages:

For Europe, kids need to be able to sit on the eight-hour flight, so I would recommend they be at least three years old for that. Don't get me wrong; I have done it with younger kids, and it is possible, just not very enjoyable. The age recommendation also depends on what you are doing once you are there. If you are going to see cities with museums, I think seven is the youngest I would recommend. If you are going hiking in the Alps or having picnics in the countryside with a few gardens thrown in, kids can be three or four. If you are just going to museums, the children need to be at least thirteen.

Interests:

This is the most challenging continent on which to entertain both kids and adults at the same time. The adults want to go to the fabulous museums and castles and eat multicourse dinners in the wonderful fine-dining restaurants. None of that will appeal to kids of almost any age. However, life is about compromises, so this is one trip where both parents and kids need to compromise.

You need to view Europe as a cultural experience for the kids, no matter what they see. They do not need to spend five hours in the Louvre, and they do not need to visit every must-see sight. You do need to take them to wax museums, aquariums, nature museums, or maybe even Euro Disney. Find things that kids like to do and mix them in with things that you like to do. You might go to a museum in the morning followed by a toy store or aquarium in the afternoon. Also, don't try to pack in too much. Figure out your kids' interests and plan on doing at least one kid-oriented thing and one adult activity each day. Kids might like:

Aquariums
Nature museums
Plays
Modern art museums
Shopping
Amusement parks
Wax museums
Toy stores
Monuments
Castles
Parks
Picnics in the country
Boat rides
Science museums
Biking or hiking

When tackling museums, don't feel that you have to see the entire museum. Do an hour at most. This gives the kids a snippet of culture without having them hate you. Make sure you get your tickets ahead of time online to avoid waiting in line for an hour. Depending how old your children are, the audio tours at museums are usually very good. You can also check out www.sound-guides.com or other audio tours available for MP3 players, iPods, etc.

There are a couple of memberships and websites to check out depending on where in Europe you are going:

www.alata.it—Prescheduled appointment for St. Mark's .
www.florenceforfun.com —Membership to museums in Florence.
www.freelondonlistings.co.uk—Free events in London.

www.royal-oak.org - Membership for entry into castles in Great Britain

www.hrp.org.uk – Discounts on admission to five of London's palaces

Family Temperament:

Any kind of family can enjoy Europe. If you want to relax, go to the mountains or the sea. If you want activity, try biking or hiking through Europe. If you like to see tourist attractions, go to the cities.

Hassle Factor:

Europe is not the easiest vacation because they have different systems and different languages, and it is far away. The flights are not the easiest because, depending where you live, they can be eight hours or more. Then you have the jet lag that makes you very tired for a few days each way. However, if you gear the trip with your family in mind, you will have a wonderful experience.

Budget:

Europe is expensive. There are ways to cut costs, but it is among the most expensive of trips. The cities are more expensive than the country. You can cut costs on accommodations, but you still have the airfare. Make your arrangements as far in advance as possible.

Accommodations:

Hotels in Europe are often small. If you have three children, it is often hard to fit in a cot. Think about whether you want to find a European-feeling hotel or a newer, more Americanized hotel. There is no right or wrong answer here. The pros to an American hotel would be that children could find food they like and watch American TV, and you could probably fit three kids in a room. If you go with the European hotel, you will get more of a flavor of the culture. Sometimes these hotels are filled with antiques, allow smoking, and serve only European food.

I have visited Europe several different ways. I have gone on our version of *European Vacation*, traveling from city to city. I have gone on a ten-day bike trip and seen the countryside of France. Many times, I have gone to one city for a week or so. If you have less than two weeks, I would try to stay put with kids and learn as much as you can about the region. It will be more enjoyable and less stressful.

Resources

To rent a French villa, visit www.abritel.fr.

Windows on Italy www.windowsonitaly.com offers luxury places to stay in Italy and other parts of Europe

Rentxpress www.rentxpress.com offers smaller rentals across the world.

TripAdvisor.com and RentVillas.com are a few others to try.

Hotels.com, Expedia.com, and all the regular sites offer hotels.

Once you find a hotel, check out the review online to see what people thought. TripAdvisor, Yelp, and the guidebooks should be a help.

Tips and Suggestions:

Do Europe in chunks rather than all of Europe in six weeks. Spend a week or two in a couple of cities or countries. This holds kids' attention better and they can tolerate seeing museums for a week. It also immerses them in the culture more than the twenty-countries-in-twenty-days trip. Start with countries that your kids have studied in school or appeal most to them.

Western Europe is a good place for families to start. The food is easy in Italy. Venice, with its gondolas, is really fun with kids. London's Tower of London, Buckingham Palace, and Big Ben are seen in many movies and are monuments children recognize. The Eiffel Tower is fun because it symbolizes France and offers panoramic city views. The castles along the Loire are good for older kids. If you have outdoorsy, energetic kids, hiking in Switzerland or Austria can also be great.

In general, I think the countryside in Europe can be easier and more relaxed than the cities. You can see how cheese or chocolate is made and have picnics, tour some castles, and get to know the culture.

Most kids are more interested in architecture than art. They really haven't studied art until college, so the history and prestige of art museums are not as interesting to most kids. They like the culture and notice things you don't, which makes traveling with them so much fun.

There are many ways to see Europe. You can go by bike, stay in a hotel, rent a chalet or villa, or take a cruise. A bike tour is fun, but you don't really get to see as many of the must-see sights. However, with kids, this might be a fun way to get exposed to a country. There are many organizations running bike trips—Butterfield & Robinson www.butterfield.com and Backroads www.backroads.com are two of the better known ones.

What to do

There are so many fun things to do in Europe that I can't begin to list them, but here are some suggestions:

England—London, countryside
France—Paris, Loire Valley, Provence
Italy—Rome, Florence, Venice, Amalfi Coast, Sicily, countryside
Greece—Athens, islands
Switzerland—Geneva, any ski resort

Food

One thing people seem to worry about is what their kids will eat in Europe. This is not a problem as long as you don't force things on them or pick restaurants that are not appropriate for kids. In France, for instance, almost every town has a bistro, which is a more casual restaurant that serves pasta, croque-monsieurs, chicken, and beef, etc. The items on the menu may be unfamiliar to your kids, but these bistros can all make grilled cheese and pasta with butter and cheese. Pizza in

Europe is different from our pizza, but sometimes it is OK. The other thing to expect in Europe is fabulous desserts.

Don't stress if for one week your kids eat more desserts than they should. If they don't eat everything on their plate, don't worry about it. Move on, and go have a crepe or french fries. Occasionally, you can even go to familiar destinations like McDonald's and Starbucks, though be aware that they serve different food and are not the same as their counterparts in the United States. View it as a cultural experience—seeing how familiar restaurants and stores are different in other countries. In general, I would just relax and not have strict rules while on vacation. I always try to get my kids to eat some new foods. Sometimes I am successful and other times not, but it is worth a try.

Cars

Some people are afraid to drive in Europe. This is with good reason, but I think a European vacation can be a lot more fun if you can venture around.

Brush up on the signage in the country you will be traveling to. Get a GPS, but also purchase a map. The GPS sometimes takes you on a very circuitous route and loses signal in cities.

You can rent cars with automatic transmissions, but not as easily as those with manual, so make sure you reserve in advance if you don't know how to drive a stick shift. The cars in Europe are generally smaller, so if yours is a big family you will have to see what is available. However, there are more big cars in Europe these days. The roads are windy and narrow, but you get used to them quickly.

Make sure you get car insurance. European drivers are good and probably better than in the United States, but they do drive fast. The highways are fast, but are smooth and not as crowded as in the United States. Cities are hardest to drive in, as they can be crowded and not clearly marked. However, if you're able to drive in any major US city, you should be fine. England is difficult because you drive on the left, but you do adjust quickly and it's good for a few laughs. Each country is a little different. Some have roundabouts that take getting used to but aren't bad once you get the hang of them. Some roads in parts of Europe are very narrow, windy, and rocky.

Active and Adventure Travel

Ages: 10 and up
Interests: Exploring, sports, culture, hiking, biking, animals, nature
Family Temperament: Outgoing, fearless, laid-back, active
Hassle Factor: High
Budget: $$$$-$$$$$

My favorite trips are the active and adventure trips because they are so unique and different from anything I do at home. My absolutely favorite place to go in the world is on safari in Kenya and Tanzania. I have been twice. Once we stayed in lodges and the other time in tents, and it is awesome either way. It is so beautiful, and seeing the animals in their natural surroundings is breathtaking. We also have loved hiking the Amazon in Peru, Macchu Picchu, and the rainforest in Costa Rica. My most memorable hike was with the mountain gorillas in Rwanda. I have fond memories of whitewater rafting with my dad on the Green River in Utah on a five-day trip. Whitewater rafting in Alaska is pretty amazing as well. These trips challenge you and allow you to experience things you wouldn't otherwise. They are truly amazing!

Ages:

As the kids get older, and depending on their interests and yours, these can be some of the best trips imaginable. These trips are fabulous, but they are not everyone's cup of tea. It would be best if you have traveled a fair amount before tackling these. For these trips I would make sure all children are at least ten years old—waiting until then will make it more fun for everyone. It's an adventure even getting to some of these places.

Interests:

Activities run the gamut from sports—like fishing, golf, biking, rock climbing, or skiing—to those dealing with culture, architecture, or nature and animals. There are trips around the world for any interest. The further from home they are, the more they become an adventure.

Family Temperament:

These are great for an active or adventurous family. Active and adventure trips can be taxing, both emotionally and physically. Not everything goes according to plan. There can be some rough spots along the way, and you need to be able to go with the flow. These are great trips if you can be patient with delayed flights, international customs, and other unknowns. You will see loads of amazing sights and lots of unbelievable things will happen. These trips really bond you as a family.

Hassle Factor:

The hassle factor can be high because often you are traveling at least eight hours from home. The plane rides can be long, and as I said earlier, not everything always goes according to plan. You have to deal with international regulations and customs, which are different from our own. Some countries have very rigid policies and others have such laid-back policies that the country is not run very efficiently. Either one can be a hassle.

Budget:

These are often the most expensive trips. The flights are expensive for starters, but the tour operators that set everything up can be pricey. The accommodations can be any price, depending if you are going for budget hotels or luxury.

Accommodations:

Accommodations can be organized through a tour operator. Otherwise, do a fair amount of research so you know what you are getting.

Tips and Suggestions:

Here are some ideas for adventure travel destinations:
North America
> Hiking or rafting the Grand Canyon
> Alaska—anything you do there is an adventure
> Horseback riding
> Fly-fishing in the West
> Snorkeling, surfing, or scuba diving in Hawaii
> Biking across the country or through one part of it
> Hiking through national parks
> Playing golf at some of the top golf courses in the country
> Heli-skiing in Western Canada
> A polar bear safari in Canada

Central and South America
> Whale watching in Mexico
> Monarch butterfly migration in Mexico
> Snorkeling or scuba diving the Barrier Reef in Belize
> Visiting the Mayan ruins of Mexico
> Hiking the rain forests of Costa Rica
> Hiking Machu Picchu in Peru
> Snorkeling in the Galapagos Islands
> Skiing in Chile
> Hiking in the Amazon rain forest

Antarctica
> Penguin viewing

Australia
> Snorkeling and scuba diving in the Great Barrier Reef
> National parks, kangaroos, and koalas

Golfing some of the top courses in the world in New Zealand and Australia

Snorkeling, culture, and beaches in Fiji, Bora Bora, and the Polynesian Islands

Asia

Hiking or biking the Great Wall of China

Horseback riding in Mongolia

Beijing, Hong Kong, Thailand, Japan

Europe

Golf in Scotland, England or Ireland

Skiing or hiking in Switzerland, France, Austria, or Italy

Arctic golf and polar bear sighting at the North Pole

Staying at the famous Ice Hotel in Sweden

Africa

Safaris in Kenya, Tanzania, Botswana, Zimbabwe, or South Africa

Great Pyramids in Egypt

Traveling down the Nile

Morocco

Snorkeling in the Seychelles

Trekking with the mountain gorillas in Rwanda or Uganda

There is an infinite amount of information and places to go, and if this appeals to you check out these adventure travel directories:

Gordon's Guide, www.gordonsguide.com

Great Outdoor Recreation Pages, www.GORP.com

Specialty Travel, www.specialtytravel.com

Check out www.7continentsclub.com to see how a family of five traveled to fifty states and seven continents over the course of five years. It is quite an inspiration.

Look at adventure travel magazines like *National Geographic Adventure* and *Outside* for ideas as well.

Some of the best tour operators are:
- Abercrombie & Kent www.abercrombiekent.com—adventure travel around the world
- Tauck www.tauck.com – expeditions around the world
- GAdventures www.gadventures.com—adventure travel at an economical price
- Butterfield & Robinson www.butterfield.com—bike trips around the world
- Big Five Tours & Expeditions www.bigfive.com—African safaris
- Ker & Downey www.ker-downeyafrica.com—luxury African safaris
- Geographic Expeditions www.geoex.com – adventure travel
- REI Adventures www.rei.com/adventures - Active trips offered by the REI Outfitters
- Backroads www.backroads.com—bike trips
- National Geographic www.nationalgeographic.com – Adventures travel around the world
- Lindblad Expeditions – www.expeditions.com – Adventurous travel to exotic places
- Adventures in Golf – www.adventures-in-golf.com – Golf trips to Scotland and England

Volunteering

Ages: 12 and up
Interests: Charity, helping others, showing your kids those less fortunate, cultural experience
Family temperament: Outgoing, adventurous, patient, charitable, laid-back
Hassle Factor: High
Budget: $$$

For the most adventurous of all, you could do a family volunteer trip. These are run by nonprofit organizations to help countries in need. This does not mean they are economical, but they can be a very fulfilling experience. They can be rustic and take hard work, but also very rewarding.

Ages:

I would recommend age twelve and up, but many of the organizations will have their own guidelines. I just think the kids need to be able to understand what they are doing to appreciate this type of trip. They also need to be able to do the physical work involved.

Interests:

This is a trip where you need to be interested in helping others. You might also be interested in exposing your kids to those less fortunate. It is a cultural experience, and therefore if you are keen on showing your kids other cultures in a less touristy fashion, this would be a very interesting way to do that.

Family Temperament:

The type of families best suited for this trip would be outgoing, adventurous, patient, charitable, and a bit laid-back. These trips can be hard work. You are going to be in the poorest parts of the country you are visiting, and you are there to help. You are not going to be catered to as you would on another type of vacation. However, you will probably feel a much deeper sense of reward and attachment than you would on any other type of trip.

Hassle Factor:

This is probably the most work and, consequently, hassle of any type of trip. You are often far from home in a third-world country. There might not be plumbing, showers, or toilets. This vacation requires a lot of manual labor. You will have to get shots and, depending on where you are going, you might have to take malaria pills. These places are often hard to get to as well. Your accommodations will be fairly basic.

Budget:

These trips are not as cheap as you would think. They are considered a charitable contribution so are priced so that the organization makes money. On top of that, you have to pay for plane tickets to get there. You have to see it as a priceless experience.

Accommodations:

The accommodations will be set up by the organization.

Tips and Suggestions:

There are two directories where you can find information:
International Volunteer Programs Association,
www.volunteerinternational.org

Volunteer Abroad, www.volunteerabroad.com

There are also organizations that specialize in volunteer travel:

Global Service Corps, www.globalservicecorps.org

Cross-Cultural Solutions, www.crossculturalsolutions.org

Earthwatch Institute, www.earthwatch.org

Global Citizens Network, www.globalcitizens.org

Oceanic Society, www.oceanicsociety.org

Sierra Club, www.sierraclub.org

Habitat for Humanity, www.habitat.org

Part III

How to Travel with Kids of All Ages

Now that you have picked a few destinations based on your interests, here are some recommendations based on the specific ages of your children. Every age group has its challenges, but with a few suggestions, you can take your children almost anywhere.

Traveling with Infants:

Destination choices

- Resort
- City
- Cruise

It's important to remember that your infant doesn't need a vacation—you do. When planning a vacation with an infant, you must consider this: What destination and travel circumstances will give you the break you want? You don't want to arrive home from your vacation stressed and tired. Traveling with an infant is going to require a lot of work and attention, so I wouldn't recommend any trip too adventurous at this age—the closer to home, the better.

All you really need for a successful, relaxing vacation with an infant is a nice place to stroll, good weather, and simple amenities. Realize that someone will need to stay with your baby at nap time, so pick a location where that is possible.

Accommodations

With infants, a hotel room is probably the easiest and most economical. They are not eating real food yet so there are not worries about restaurant meals or anything of that nature. They can sleep on the floor, in a crib, or just about anywhere.

I always tried to find someplace with a pool since I like to swim and had my kids in the pool at about three months old.

Activities

Strolling, playing in the sand, and swimming with Mom and Dad are activities you might do at a resort. You can also take an infant to a museum, out to eat, or visit a zoo, aquarium, or anything else in a city. Relaxing by the pool on a cruise and sightseeing would be fun too. Since infants are still sleeping a lot, the activities are limited in length, but you can take most infants anywhere.

Preparing for the trip

All you have to do is book your trip with the resort, cruise, or hotel and purchase some plane tickets. None of the activities should have to be booked ahead of time. Keep it simple.

Packing

The smaller the child, the more stuff he or she requires. At this age you will be hauling car seats, strollers, diaper bags, toys, books, a change of clothes, snacks, etc. wherever you go. Packing as light as possible is key to no-hassle traveling. Diapers, for example, can take up a great deal of room, so bring enough diapers for two days and then buy the rest when you arrive. Babies' clothes are tiny, so don't skimp there. Bring enough for two to three changes per day. Infants constantly throw up or soil their clothes so that is not where to cut back.

On the plane

Infants are actually easier on the plane than toddlers. I would recommend always getting them their own seat. My youngest child never slept until the plane landed, but if he had his own seat he was much calmer and could at least be entertained. A lot of kids don't want to be held for over an hour. My independent daughter hated sitting on my lap. The goal with infants is to get them to sleep on the plane; the chances of this are better if they have their own seat. Add to this the common occurrences of flights being delayed, infants being naturally squirmy, and other unexpected casualties—it is easier on everyone if babies have their own seat, and much safer as well.

If your infant sleeps on the plane, you are in great shape. However, if you have a long flight and the infant has to sit still, you will have to entertain him or her for the duration of the flight. My doctor recommended giving babies Dramamine, but I never found this to work. It would only make them tired once we landed. With infants, hopefully you won't be traveling more than a few hours.

Final considerations

My oldest was extremely energetic, screamed a lot, and barely ever sat still. My daughter was definitely easier as a baby. She would sit still pretty well, and we could take her anywhere and she would be content. My youngest—and it is probably because he is the youngest—would go with the flow for the most part. However, he is the one who would throw Hot Wheels and get sick on the airplanes. So when thinking about your trip, what to bring, and where to go, you really need to consider the temperament of the baby.

You also need to consider your own temperament. How easily do you get stressed, and how tolerant are you of a few bumps in the road? Do you experience more stress on city streets or when you're in nature? This will help guide you on where you should go and how difficult a trip you should consider.

Traveling with Two- to Five-Year-Olds:

Destination Choices

- Beach resort
- Mountains
- National park
- Disney World or other amusement park

At this age, I would pick places that are easy and relaxing. I wouldn't even recommend Disney World until age four or five. Many people take infants and two-year-olds there and it is too overwhelming, crowded, and tiring. They can't do a lot of the rides and need to take naps. They would be much better off at a beach vacation. You can do summer in the mountains where the little ones can run around, and it is casual and not too expensive. A ski vacation is also fun, and at about four or five they can begin to learn to ski.

Accommodations

At this age I would highly recommend getting a condo. Young children do not like sitting for long meals in restaurants. It is much easier to have a kitchen so you can give them a quick breakfast and a dinner they'll like.

Since children this age will still be taking naps, it is also nice to have accommodations with a living room and separate bedrooms. This enables someone to sit and read while the child takes a nap in peace and quiet.

Activities

Kids can start to do a lot more activities at this age. Obviously, a beach and a pool are great. In addition, they can start to play tennis, ski, and hike. Disney World and other amusement parks are lots of fun for four- and five-year-olds. This is a really great age because they can do a lot of different activities as long as there isn't too much sitting or being quiet involved.

Preparing for the trip

With younger children, you are likely not yet tied to any school schedule, so you can go on vacation any time. It is cheaper if you can avoid travel during school holidays or big national holidays. You will need to make your plane ticket and an accommodation arrangement ahead of time, but nothing else needs much organization. If you go to a ski resort, you might have to sign up for ski school in advance. During peak seasons do this early, but otherwise a few weeks before should be fine.

Packing

Bring lots of entertainment and snacks. At this age it is better to overpack than be caught unprepared. I used to be a real old-fashioned mom and refuse to bring a DVD player, but I have broken down in my old age—if you want any time to yourself, it can be a real lifesaver. I still don't let my kids watch the DVD player all the way to Peru; however, use your own judgment and just know that it is a good option. In addition, for a big trip I pack a little surprise bag of new toys, cards, cars, coloring books, games, snacks, etc. depending on the kids' ages. It is always fun and entertaining to have something new to surprise them with.

On the plane

This age group can be more challenging than the infants because they actually can move and get into things. Plane rides are especially challenging. They are supposed to sit still and will want to do anything except that. I remember trying to wear out my oldest son before boarding many planes by walking and running around the airport. I don't think it ever worked. He was very energetic; plane rides were exhausting for me as I tried my best to entertain him in a seated position. My other son constantly threw Hot Wheels at the other passengers, so I learned not to bring small toys on board. It is a wonder that I continued my quest to see the world with those two! So my first bit of advice is: find places with short travel times, whether by car, train, or plane.

Also, consider the temperament of your children. My daughter was much more mild-mannered and easier to fly with than my sons, so I could have flown anywhere with her. My youngest son got sick on planes, and I didn't know that until his first flight to Europe. So be prepared for the worst. Bring extra clothes for you and your child, if possible.

Final considerations

This can be an exhausting age, so keep it as simple and relaxing as possible. Also, make sure you fit in time for Mom and Dad. Hire a babysitter one or two nights so you can have some alone time. Schedule a spa treatment or go play a game of tennis. Divide and conquer or hire some help. You might bring a babysitter or most places will be able to arrange one for you.

Traveling with Five- to Eight-Year-Olds:

Destinations

- Resorts
- Mountains
- Cities
- Cruises
- National parks
- Disney World
- Europe

Traveling with this age group should still be about what you want to do while keeping it pretty simple. I think this is a great age for national parks or someplace casual. You don't want anyplace with long, formal dinners; kids have no interest in that and can't sit for that long. They like to run around and not be told to be quiet. I like the national parks because the children can run around, see things, and use up energy. Everything is extremely cheap and casual.

Ski vacations are great because if you want your kids to learn to ski, the earlier the better. However, ski trips are exhausting for parents. Sometimes the kids hate ski school, so you have to negotiate that one. The parents have to carry all the skis and get everyone dressed with all that equipment and it is hard to walk in the ski boots. Now, I didn't grow up in a skiing family so it was all new to me, but my husband has always been an avid skier, so we have had the kids skiing since about age four. I always felt like I needed a vacation from my vacation afterward. However, my kids are now great skiers and can carry their own skis so it has turned into a fun family vacation. It really is beautiful, and I pick ski resorts where there are things to do besides skiing, and I have a great time too.

Kids are pretty energetic at this age, so I like trips in the countryside or mountains or anything in the outdoors. This is not the best age for museums or anything fancy. You can do Europe, but make it hiking in the mountains or something in the country. Tropical beaches are great, and even some of the more adventurous travel is good for seven- to eight-year-olds.

Accommodations

Children in this age group can be picky eaters, so I still suggest a condo over a hotel room unless you are in a city and have no other option. I like being able to eat at the condo because most kids this age still don't like sitting for a lengthy meal. I also like to spread out in the afternoon for a game of Apples to Apples, Rat-a-Tat Cat, or Slamwich.

Activities

Now you can do any activity imaginable to some extent, including tennis, golf, skiing, or any other sport. Some kids are up for horseback riding, canoeing, and rafting. Sightseeing, hiking, and rides at amusement parks work too. Children's museums are great, but I would not tackle art museums quite yet.

Preparing for the trip

This is an age where you can start to explain where you are going and give them a little education ahead of time. Obviously, you need to gear your lesson toward their level of understanding, but it does make the trip more interesting and enjoyable. If you are going to New York, you can tell them that there are going to be tall buildings, and if you are going to the mountains, you can talk about that. Read some children's books about the area if you can.

Depending on where you are going, you will want to make some arrangements ahead of time. Flights and accommodations are always best reserved far in advance. You will not need to make dinner reservations since most casual restaurants do not require them. If you are going on a cruise, you will want to book the excursions well in advance. Ski school reservations need to be made in advance as well.

Packing

At this age you can have children pack their own carry-ons. This starts their independence as a traveler. However, you should check to make sure they brought what you think they need. You can give them a list to follow or suggest some items. Make sure carry-ons are light enough for children to haul on their own.

When packing, the lighter the better. Children will need to bring a variety of clothes, which makes it more difficult to pack light. However, when a whole family is traveling, it is much easier if you don't all have steamer trunks to pull off the carousel at baggage claim and load in the rental car.

On the plane

At about age four, kids become much better on long plane rides. All of a sudden, they can sit for long periods of time—they can read, play games, watch a DVD, or work a video game. They can entertain themselves much better, so distance is no longer a problem.

Final considerations

This is when traveling with children becomes a joy. Go see what they want to see. Don't try to push anything too adult and boring on them. Take them to see all the different parts of the world, but still keep it simple and fun. Have picnics in Switzerland, go to the top of the Willis Tower in Chicago, or look down at the Grand Canyon. Try skiing, a cruise in South America, or go to Disney World. You will have fun anywhere you go.

.

Traveling with Eight-to Twelve-Year-Olds

Destinations

- Resort
- Mountains
- City
- Cruise
- National park
- Disney
- Europe
- Adventure
- Volunteer

This is a really important age to travel with children. You can open up their eyes to the world and they can now comfortably travel to any destination you can think of. At the same time, they also still love you and love traveling with their family. They haven't gotten to the stage where Mom and Dad are no longer cool and don't know anything.

You can go anywhere in the world. You can start on adventure trips at this age, as most kids are able to hike for long periods of time. If you go to Europe, your kids will have studied in school a little of what they'll see on the trip so they'll have some understanding of it. You can go on safari in Africa and they will understand the cultural differences between there and home. They still enjoy the beach, but now they can play golf and tennis, they can surf and snorkel. They will also enjoy the mountains, cruises, and national parks.

I would recommend venturing beyond the resort and Disney World vacations. If possible, expand their horizons. Try different countries and experience new activities and cultures.

Accommodations

At this age, kids do start to understand the differences between a Four Seasons and a Motel 6. I still don't recommend hotels as much as condos for families, but sometimes they are the only option and are cheaper. At this age, children can start to sit at dinner without disrupting the whole restaurant, but watch out for those dinner bills. Hotels in general charge a lot for breakfast, lunch, and dinner.

Activities

Any activity is possible. Kids can now do any sport, see any sight, and eat any food. They can go on safari, hike the Grand Canyon, snorkel in the Great Barrier Reef, find the *Mona Lisa* in the Louvre, and ski the Alps. They can bike around France, find the queen's jewels, and hop in a gondola. They can ride horses, golf, play tennis, and see any museum in the world. The possibilities are endless.

Preparing for the trip

The best way to prepare for a trip with children this age is get them engaged. Have them learn about where they are going and what they want to see. My parents made my brother, sister, and me write a report on Europe beforehand. You can at least read about the countries or cities or sites you will see. Ask the kids what they would like to see or do and let each of them pick at least one site or activity.

Packing

Finally, the kids can pack their own suitcases. Make them a list and let them pack. You know your kids and will know whether you need to double-check what they've packed. Give them some independence and give yourself a break from having to do all the work for everyone.

On the plane

By now, the kids all probably have phones, books, and iPads. Throw in a few simple games, some magazines, and a journal and you should be good. Bring snacks because well-fed children are happy children.

Final considerations

You can decide whether the children will all sit together or in a different seating arrangement. At this point, my kids like sitting by themselves and my husband and I sit together.

Give each child a job for the trip, a camera, and a journal. One child can be in charge of restaurants and another museums. Or take turns with who gets to pick the restaurant. Before you leave, give everyone a job and an allowance.

Traveling with Teens

Destinations

- Resort
- Mountains
- City
- Cruise
- National park
- Disney
- Europe
- Adventure
- Volunteer

When your children enter their teens, there are now fewer opportunities for vacation. You have to work around the kids' school vacation schedule—unfortunately, these are peak travel times, which means they are expensive. Your kids' opinions are very strong when it comes to their vacation, and they can be very vocal.

Teen's friends and their opinions are very important.. At this age, your vacation becomes just as crucial to their image as what they wear, where they live, and what size their house is. It is now harder to get them to a rustic lodge in the middle of Yosemite while their friends are staying at the Four Seasons in Maui.

This is a great time to show them a variety of countries and places. However, they may not be up for traveling with their family as much as they used to. You could also take fewer, but more exotic vacations that everyone will appreciate and enjoy.

Accommodations

All of a sudden, your kids are big. It becomes harder to fit three in a hotel room. They might do some activities on their own. They can go out on their own a little, so either a hotel or a condo is fine. You don't need to cook for them and will probably enjoy going out as a family. You do not have to have a living room for reading and games, and they kind of like having their independence. Hotels require one adult per room, but you know your family and how to split up best.

Activities

Again, any activity is possible. Teenagers can do any sport, eat any food, go to any museum, and see any site. Do whatever piques their interest and combine it with what you want them to do. The more input you get from them, the less they will dread the trip.

At this age, kids might not be open to as many options. They might not want to go to museums, national parks, or ski trips. They have strong opinions, likes and dislikes. Find out what they want to do and make sure there is something for everyone to please the whole family

Preparing for the trip

Involve your kids. Ask the kids what they want to do and see.

Packing

The kids can certainly pack. Make sure you emphasize what you want them to wear or bring. They can be forgetful or have selective memory. If you want them to bring dress shoes, you might have to remind them three times.

On the plane

Teens can take care of their carry-ons. Just tell them how long the flight will be and they should know what to bring. They know how to download movies. Remind them to bring a few fun games and books.

Final considerations

This is an important time to bond with your kids, and when traveling you do have their undivided attention. They can't shut the door or spend all day in front of the computer or at their friend's house. They have to deal with you and talk to you. Get them out of their comfort zone and do something as a family. It is the best thing for everyone. My advice is to listen as they tell you where they want to go and what they want to do. Compromise, and if you want to take them to Europe then you really should go to Orlando or Maui or wherever they want to go too. Maybe everyone gets to pick one vacation spot for the year. You can even give them the budget and let them figure it out. They are probably more savvy on the computer than you are. Another idea is to give them a list of possibilities and let them choose. Let them think they are in control. Keep the relationship strong and realize that it is not always smooth sailing, but it is just a phase.

Traveling for All Ages:

I have always based my family vacation decisions on the abilities of my oldest child—I think this is because my youngest is a more laid-back kind of kid who can go with the flow. Also, my husband and I sometimes do split up. When the youngest was a toddler, my husband would take the older two kids whitewater rafting while I sat with my youngest so he could nap. We went to Alaska when my kids were ten, eight, and five years old. It was fine, but there were certainly things the youngest couldn't do that the older two could. As long as you are willing to compromise like that, you will be fine. This also depends on the age spread of your children. I have a five-year spread between my oldest and youngest. If you have much more than that, or you have a larger family, you might have to base your vacation choices on what the youngest can do or take separate trips occasionally.

To summarize, I have made this chart for review and simplification:

	Resort	Mountains	Cruise	National Park	City	Disney	Europe	Active/ Adventure	Volunteer
Ages									
Baby	✓			✓					
Toddler	✓			✓					
4-8	✓	✓	✓	✓	✓	✓	✓		
9-12	✓	✓	✓	✓	✓	✓	✓	✓	
Teens	✓	✓	✓	✓	✓	✓	✓	✓	✓
Interests									
Outdoors	✓	✓		✓			✓	✓	✓
Culture	✓		✓		✓		✓	✓	✓
Sports	✓	✓		✓			✓	✓	
Relaxation	✓		✓				✓		
Entertainment			✓		✓	✓	✓		
Nature		✓		✓			✓	✓	✓
Temperament									
Laid-back	✓	✓	✓	✓	✓		✓	✓	✓
Moderate	✓	✓	✓	✓	✓	✓	✓	✓	✓
Energetic	✓	✓		✓			✓	✓	✓
Hassle Factor									
Low	✓		✓	✓					
Medium					✓	✓	✓		
High		✓						✓	✓
Budget									
$	✓		✓	✓					
$$	✓		✓	✓	✓				
$$$	✓	✓	✓		✓	✓			✓
$$$$	✓	✓			✓	✓	✓	✓	✓
$$$$$							✓	✓	

Once you have narrowed down a few choices, use my calculator in Appendix B to make sure you can stay within your budget.

Part IV

Planning and Organizing a Great Trip

Making the Reservations

Certain things need to be done far in advance and others can be done last minute. In order to organize your time, here is what needs to be done when:

Six months or more in advance:
- Purchase plane tickets
- Book hotel or condo
- Passports, Visas and shots

One month in advance:
- Reserve rental car
- Schedule any activities
- Make dinner reservations
- Schedule golf tee times, tennis court reservations, spa appointments, ski school or instructors
- Order tickets to museums or shows and schedule a guide if needed
- Schedule kennel for your dog if you have one

One week in advance:
- Pack
- Confirm that flight times have not changed
- Order transportation to and from airport if necessary
- Send anything you will need (golf clubs, skis, etc.)
- Order diapers, groceries, etc. to be delivered at destination
- Check seating arrangement
- Buy anything you will need for trip including special clothes, toiletries, games
- Stop mail and newspapers for vacation hold

The day before:
- Check in with the airline online
- Pack carry-on
- Pack all paperwork
- Pack guidebooks
- Go to the bank
- Call credit card companies to let them know you will be traveling

The day of travel:
- Wear comfortable clothes
- Make sure you have tickets, passports, driver's licenses, and other paperwork
- Bring a coat, if necessary
- Don't forget anyone's suitcase
- Give the kids money or budget for the trip
- Determine seating arrangement on the plane
- Leave lots of extra time to get to the airport, check-in, buy snacks, etc.

Plane tickets

I would recommend making plane reservations as far in advance as possible. Airlines usually allow you to book flights eleven months in advance. You get a better fare, generally, when you book in advance. Once you determine where you are going, you can see which airlines fly into the closest airport. One thing to consider is that smaller airports are often much easier and less time-consuming than large airports. However, larger airports can be less expensive. Not as many flights will fly in and out of small airports, though, so if you miss your flight or you get bumped or anything goes wrong, it will be a while until there is another plane. At a large airport, there are usually hourly flights. I used to always use Expedia to determine which airline flies where at what price, but they don't include Southwest Airlines, so you will have to do a little more work to see who is flying where and when.

Frequent flyer programs

If you travel a lot or plan to, sign everyone up for a frequent flyer program with one of the major airlines. For every fifty thousand miles, you will receive a free domestic ticket. You can also sign up for a credit card that earns miles on that airline. United and American are two of the most popular. If you keep flying the same airline, you will rack up the most miles and get more free tickets. You can also use the miles for upgrades to business or first class.

Check out the programs at
www.united.com
www.aa.com
www.southwest.com
www.delta.com

Lounges

You might consider joining one of the nice lounges the airlines offer. American has the Admirals Club, United has the Red Carpet Room, and Delta has their Sky Club. The lounge access costs several hundred dollars per year, but if you are traveling a lot with children, they are nice. They offer Wi-Fi, snacks, TV, a bar, and comfortable seating.

Plane ticket checklist

If you do not need to be loyal to one airline:

- Check prices on Kayak, which will compare rates from Expedia, Priceline, Hotwire, Orbitz, and CheapOair
- Check prices on airlines' websites
- Check Southwest Airlines since they are not on the other search sites
- Consider schedule as well as price
- Reserve seats, if possible
- Use miles, if applicable

Tips

- Avoid very short layovers and extremely long layovers
- Don't schedule flights before 9:00 a.m. or after 9:00 p.m. when traveling with a family
- Shorter flights and drives are better, especially for younger children
- Seats are generally better when purchasing flights directly from the airline
- Buy a seat for everyone (even infants)
- Select seats that are together
- Pay for extra legroom if you have tall teenagers (or adults) and are traveling more than three hours
- Sign up for a mileage program and stick to one airline, or get a credit card that allows you to use points toward any airline

When making your reservation, you also might consider the on-time record of the airline, their policies, and which airlines fly direct to your destination. The bigger the airline, the more chances for things to go wrong, so they are less likely to be on time and more likely to lose luggage. Airlines differ on some of their policies, including whether children can travel alone, how far in advance you must check in, and baggage fees. Always check the airline's policies online if in doubt.

You might decide to use miles you have accrued with the airline either through your credit card or by flying frequently. You can generally use these toward a free ticket or for an upgraded seat. Each airline has different policies as to how many miles you need for a free ticket and how many miles you need for an upgrade. Seats these days seem to offer less and less legroom. I used to always go for the free ticket, but I recently booked a flight to Hawaii from Chicago and went for the upgrade to business class. I would say that if you are making a long-distance flight of more than four hours, I would now elect to upgrade. However, this depends on your budget, your height, and the ages of the children you are traveling with.

When making your reservation, if possible fly on off-days and at off-times of the year. If you are flexible, fly during the middle of the week and not during Thanksgiving or Winter break. However, once your kids are in school, there is nothing you can do about this, so you just have to be prepared. Allow extra time at the airport and expect lost luggage as part of the trade-off of vacation travel.

Hotel or condo

The decision on whether to stay in a hotel or condo depends on the ages of the children and their ability to sit at restaurants for meals. In most cases, with children age two through eighteen, a condo is better. If you have only one child under the age of two, a hotel would probably be just fine. If you have teenagers and you like to go out for your meals, then a hotel will be OK. However, for the majority a condo is better. It allows the kids to have more room to roam, and if they are a little noisy, you don't have to worry about the neighbors on the other side of the wall.

Renting a condo is also easier for meals. My kids were (and still are) picky eaters. For example, if the pizza at the restaurant comes back with oregano sprinkled on top, they won't eat it. If a restaurant forgets to take the pickles and onions off a burger, we always have to send it back. On top of that, dining out can be expensive, depending on where you are staying. We recently found a really good hotel deal at the Ritz-Carlton in Jamaica. However, we spent $200 at every meal—there were no other restaurants nearby—so it didn't turn out to be such a good deal.

I find condos or houses with a kitchen are ideal. It is easier to fix breakfast and dinner when your kids want to eat and to make what they want. Going out to long meals with little kids is not an option unless you have an extremely placid child. It is also better if the child has his own room, so he can nap and go to bed when he needs to, not when you do. Also, when he is napping, you can be in the living room watching TV or reading a book, not sitting right next to him in a hotel room with two beds.

I find that it is much easier to find the right hotel than condo. Websites such as Expedia, Orbitz, and TripAdvisor rank the hotels and have customer reviews, and from them you know the difference between a Four Seasons, a Marriott, and a Best Western. You can book the hotel either directly or on Expedia, Hotels.com, or any of the online booking agencies.

The problem with condos is they are usually run out of the resort, and it is hard to tell what you are going to get ahead of time. I have not found an agency to rank rental condos, and there is no overall brand name associated with them. They are often not as nice as hotels—however, for kids they are much better. Now, some resorts offer condos on their property. So you could stay at a Hyatt in Puerto Rico, for example, and they would have both hotel rooms and condos. Then you would sort of know what to expect. However, if you go to Vail and want to stay at a condo, it is hard to know what you will get. There are nice ones, crummy ones, and everything in between. You also don't know how the location will be. Some condos are pretty awful. I would try to stay at a resort where you either have a personal recommendation or you know what to expect. Every time I have stayed at a random condo, I have been disappointed. This is why the vacation clubs have done so well.

If you are going to go with a condo, ask a lot of questions. I have rented condos thinking I was getting a kitchen and just got a mini-fridge. TripAdvisor is another Internet source for information. Get recommendations from friends and family. Read reviews before making your reservation.

Following are some websites to contact:
www.cyberrentals.com
www.windowsonitaly.com
www.greatrentals.com
www.rentalo.com
www.vrbo.com
www.vacationrentals.com
www.tripadvisor.com
You can also call the local real estate agent for vacation rentals.

Why vacation clubs are great for families

Vacation clubs are my new favorite thing. Vacation clubs are essentially luxury timeshares. The most popular are Exclusive Resorts, Four Seasons, and Ritz-Carlton. You join for a fee and there are annual dues. You are given a certain number of days per year. Then you are allowed a certain number of holiday vacations, which are during spring break, Fourth of July, and Thanksgiving. You can book at any of their locations all over the world. My family was one of the original members of Exclusive Resorts. In the first couple of years, it was possible to book any property you wanted whenever you wanted. Now, as more people have joined, it is much more difficult. The timeshares are all beautiful and in great locations. I have never been disappointed. Now, these would not be appropriate if you cannot plan far in advance or want to go someplace specific. Often you have to take what is available. The clubs can be expensive and have restrictions. However, the accommodations are always nice and are worth checking into.

You should check out these programs and websites:
Exclusive Resorts, www.exclusiveresorts.com
Four Seasons, www.residences.fourseasons.com
Ritz-Carlton, www.ritzcarltonclub.com

These are in the top tier. Marriott, Hilton, Sheraton, and Hyatt offer them too, as do many individual hotels, such as the Franz Klammer Lodge in Telluride, Colorado.

Check out:
Hilton, www.hiltongrandvacations.com
Hyatt, www.hyattvacationclub.com
Sheraton, www.sheratonvacationownership.com
Marriott, www.marriottvacationclub.com

There are many, many others, plus websites to compare the different programs. Each program has different levels of membership, so this is just a starting point. Another advantage, besides knowing what level of accommodations you will get, is that the vacation clubs are a terrific way to see many different places.

Accommodations checklist:

- Condo or hotel
- Check out reviews on TripAdvisor, Yelp, and other critiques

- Read guidebook suggestions
- Talk to friends for recommendations
- Read travel magazines for suggestions

International Travel

Plane tickets

In addition to the websites mentioned in the plane ticket section, check out the following:

www.opodo.co.uk
www.openjet.com
www.applefares.com
www.skyscanner.net
www.whichbudget.com

Accommodations

Again, there are some websites dedicated to international accommodations.

Check out the following:
www.windowsonitaly.com www.rentalo.com
www.vrbo.com

Paperwork and shots

When traveling abroad, check the legal requirements in each country. Shots and visas are required to enter some countries and notarized letters are required if both legal parents are not accompanying the children.

- Check the US Centers for Disease Control website for required shots at www.cdc.gov

- Make sure passports are up to date. Passports are required for everyone, even if the baby is a week old. Information can be accessed at www.travel.state.gov/passport
- Check the country website for visa requirements or check www.travel.state.gov/visa

Phones

In Europe it is cheaper to buy a phone at your destination so that you don't get a huge bill for roaming charges when you get home. Another option is to pay for international service on your own phone; if you do this, turn off the roaming feature and don't check e-mail too often.

One Month in Advance

One month in advance you should:

- Reserve rental car
- Schedule any activities
- Make dinner reservations
- Schedule golf tee times, tennis court reservations, spa appointments, ski school or instructors
- Order tickets to museums or shows and schedule a guide if needed
- Schedule kennel for your dog if you have one

Rental cars

This is pretty straightforward. You can again search on Expedia or similar websites that compare the offerings of various car rental companies. Avis and Hertz tend to be closer to the terminal, so if you have little kids and don't want to take the shuttle bus, this might be worth the extra cost.

I would recommend signing up for a premier program so you don't have to wait in the long lines at the rental car counter. You will be dropped off at the area with available cars, you'll pick one out, and off you'll go. Waits at rental car counters can be thirty minutes or more in some busy airports. Premier programs typically offer 10 percent or more off and give you coupons and other benefits. Membership does mean you'll need to be loyal to one company. So if you are very price-conscious, this might not be your best bet. However, if your time and sanity are important, I would highly recommend this option.

I generally do not take out the extra insurance, but pay with my American Express card. The credit card company should cover any accidents, but always check to confirm what they'll cover. Recently someone hit my parked rental car in a parking lot and the damage was $500.

This was less than the deductible for my auto insurance, and American Express covered all but $50.

Also, my husband or I go separately to get the car while the rest of the family waits for the bags. This speeds up the departure from the airport. Otherwise, you have to wait for the bags, drag all the bags onto the bus, and then pick up the car. I have found it easier to have one adult and the kids wait for the bags and take them out to the curb while the other adult gets the car. Again, it depends on the size of the airport and how far away the rental cars are. If they are really far away, it might be worth dragging all the kids and luggage with you, but in most cases it's not.

When you return the rental car, again, if you have little kids and many bags, see if you can drop off the kids and bags and one parent while the other then drops off the car and takes the shuttle back to the airport.

A few preferred car rental programs

National's Emerald Isle program is free. Check it out at www.nationalcar.com.

The Hertz #1 Club program has four different levels. The first is free, the next is $60, and after that you get upgrades to the next levels with ten and forty car rentals per year. Then you get upgrades to the next car class and other benefits. Check them out at www.hertz.com.

Avis's Preferred Service program is free and allows you to skip lines. They have another program for those who rent with them twelve times per year. Check them out at www.avis.com.

Try these sites to compare prices:
Costco, www.costco.com
Priceline, www.priceline.com
Expedia, www.expedia.com
Budget, www.budget.com
Enterprise, www.enterprise.com
Dollar, www.dollar.com

Gas

Don't let the car rental company charge you for gas at their exorbitant fees. You will have a choice of prepaying and bringing the car back empty or refilling it yourself and bringing it back full. It is better to bring the tank back full. It is too hard to estimate how many miles it will take to bring it back empty.

Once you find the company you like, if you travel frequently I would advise sticking to them and skipping the lines.

Other Tips:

• You should not take out the extra insurance unless you are not covered with your own auto insurance or your credit card.
• Get the GPS, but bring a map as well. Sometimes the GPS takes you on the most circuitous routes and looking at a map can help you find the highways and most direct routes.
• International rental car companies will require you to take out insurance.

Rental car checklist:

• Reserve rental car
• Sign up for preferred rental program to save time at check-in
• Determine what size car you will need
• Determine whether you need an automatic or manual (stick shift)
• Decide whether you will prepay the gas for return
• Determine which extras you'll need, such as GPS, baby seat, ski rack
• Determine if you'll need the rental company's insurance coverage (check with your insurance company to see what is already covered)

Activities

Determine the activities options at your destination.

- Check guidebooks—Fodor's, Frommer's, Blue Planet, and others
- Google "Top ten things to do with kids in____(destination)"
- Check with your hotel's concierge
- Ask friends

Information on your destination

You can download tons of information about your destination onto your phone or computer. If you are going to Florence, for example, you can download movies, maps, and information on what to see, the history of Florence, and so on. Look at www.italyguides.it as well as iPhone apps. You can also get subway maps for almost any city at www.isubwaymaps.com. Google your destination and see what downloads are available, and also check your phone's apps. You might use a GPS feature on your phone or a portable GPS to find your way around.

Once you know your options, finalize your choices:

- Mix kids' activities with culture to ensure there is something for everyone
- Consider what your family likes to do
- Ask the kids what they want to do
- Come up with a tentative plan

	AM	PM
Day 1		
Day 2		
Day 3		
Day 4		
Day 5		
Day 6		
Day 7		

Schedule only one activity in the morning and another in the afternoon. Play the rest by ear and have a list of possibilities. Schedule some down time and just enjoy the vacation.

Dinner reservations

I would make dinner reservations if you want a fancier restaurant or it is a busy time of year. Otherwise, you can just wander around and find a place. Restaurants that take reservations tend to be nicer, but sometimes you might just want a casual pizza place. Depending on the ages of your kids, sometimes the more casual, the better. Other times, with slightly older kids who can sit for a while, you want a nice dinner. If you are looking for a nicer spot, always make a reservation. You can always cancel it later if you don't need it. During busy seasons, restaurants get crowded; you don't want to be waiting for an hour with kids for a table. Here are some handy restaurant resources:

www.menupages.com—menus of nearby restaurants
www.opentable.com—make a reservation at a restaurant
www.urbanspoon.com—restaurants in the area
Check with the concierge for recommendations.

Golf tee times, tennis court reservations, and spa appointments

Tee times are best made several weeks in advance unless you are going to Pebble Beach or other destination courses, in which case you'll often need to make those six months in advance. On the other hand, if you are just playing a regular public course, you can probably wait until the week before. To be on the safe side, I would recommend booking tee times a month in advance. Tennis courts and spas also book up quickly so reservations and appointments should be made a month in advance to avoid disappointment. You will also want to book tickets to shows, museums, or other events in advance.

Tickets & Guides

If you need tickets for anything or want to schedule a guide this is a good time to do that. You want to make sure you don't get shut out of theater tickets or a museum. Also a guide should be available if needed. Your concierge should be able to arrange all this.

Kennel

If you have a dog or any other pet make sure to schedule a reservation for them. One time I left this to the last minute and really had to scramble to find anything. Especially at busy times kennels really really book up.

The Week Before You Go

The week before you go:

- Pack
- Confirm that flight times have not changed
- Order transportation to and from airport if necessary
- Send anything you will need (golf clubs, skis, etc.)
- Order diapers, groceries, etc. to be delivered at destination
- Check plane seat arrangement to make sure they are together
- Buy anything you will need for trip, including special clothes, toiletries, games

Packing

I used to be a heavy packer, and I still pack too much. I would pack anything I might possibly need on my family's vacation, thinking: What if it's cold? What if I get invited to something fancy? What if I get sick? I would pack my salon shampoo, my aspirin, my suntan lotion, and everything I could think of. I would stick it all in my big duffel and be all set. Now, this philosophy of packing is fine if you don't mind paying the luggage fee, if you don't have to lift the suitcase, and if you don't mind the risk of it getting lost, since the airlines may leave some luggage behind if the aircraft needs to lighten its load. However, I am not up for that risk any more.

If you are a good packer, you can carry your bags onto your flight and not risk losing luggage. I have my small carry-on with wheels. Each airline has slightly different requirements, but you are generally allowed to carry on a forty-five-inch linear suitcase. This means that the height plus width plus depth can total no more than forty-five inches. What I have done recently is leave all shampoos, moisturizers, and soaps behind, figuring that a few days of hotel shampoos and soaps won't kill me. I would also recommend sending skis, golf clubs, or any large items ahead. These can get lost and now that the airline charges extra anyway, you might as well send them and be guaranteed they will be waiting at your destination. It is usually about $75 to ship within the United States.

Carry on if:

- You are traveling with children over seven
- Your trip is less than four days
- You don't want to pay the airline's fee for each bag
- You can send stuff ahead of time
- You won't have to lug your bags very far

Check bags if:

- You need to juggle small children and strollers
- You have too much stuff to carry on
- There is no fee
- You can risk losing the suitcase for a day or two
- You have too many liquids
- It is easier for you
- You are going for more than three or four days

Remember that to carry on, your bag must fit in the overhead of the plane and contain no liquids, and you must be able to lift it. One option would be to bring one carry-on bag for the family and check the rest, or vice versa.

If you are going somewhere for a week or more, and cannot fit everything into a carry-on, you have two choices, depending on your destination. You can send the extra baggage ahead of time by UPS or pack a carry-on with necessities and check a larger bag through. With the latter, you will have the essentials and won't have to sleep in your clothes for two days or more. Obviously, if you are leaving the country, it would be too expensive to ship stuff ahead of time. In that case, you want to check a larger bag but also have a small carry-on.

I have lost my bags going to the Bahamas, Florida, Kenya, Telluride, and Rome. Some were lost for a day and others a week. You have to decide how much risk you will take and how much of an inconvenience it will be for you. It's easy to buy a swimsuit but not as easy to buy ski clothes for the whole family.

In the Appendix you will find a packing list of some of the things you will need for your trip, as well as suggestions for entertainment. I would put this on your computer and print it out with the appropriate quantities. When your kids get old enough, let them pack for themselves after you give them the list. However, you should double-check what they have packed.

Confirm flights

You should definitely confirm flights. Flight information can change from the time you book the flight to the time you leave, so make sure you check departure times before leaving home. Also, if you didn't get seat assignments when you originally booked the flight, you can do that at this time.

Some airlines will offer you options, such as more legroom, access to executive lounges, priority security lines, etc. You should weigh these options. My opinion is that if you will be flying for more than three hours or are extremely long-legged, opt for more legroom if your budget allows it. If you have a long layover, I would splurge for the executive lounge. With snacks and TV, they are much more comfortable than the regular waiting areas. I would pay for priority security during busy times when you know lines will be long and you might miss a flight. Thanksgiving, Christmas, and Fourth of July are examples when priority security might be worth it.

Arrange transportation to and from the airport

Make sure you call a taxi or limo if you need one to get to and from the airport. If you are traveling at an extremely busy time of year, you might even do this further in advance, but a week is generally fine.

Send anything you will need (golf clubs, skis, etc.)

There are companies that will do this for you. UPS and FedEx are fine too. If you do this in advance, it won't cost you so much.

Order diapers, groceries, etc. to be delivered at destination

You can have all your groceries or baby stuff delivered to your condo prior to your arrival. This will save you a trip to the grocery.

Check seats

Make sure all your seats are together. This is helpful if you are traveling with young children or infants. It is best if you can do this ahead of time instead of at the airport. If you are not together, people will usually move to accommodate you, but it is easier if this is taken care of beforehand.

Buy anything you will need for trip, including special clothes, toiletries, games

You might need something special for your trip, such as hiking boots, safari clothes, a new bathing suit, etc. You might also need travel-size toiletries. I always think it is a good idea to have some new toys or books for the kids on the plane. This shopping can be done the week before or maybe a little earlier, if you want.

Have the mail and newspapers put on vacation hold.

Make sure you remember to put these on hold so that they don't pile up making it obvious that you are away.

The Day Before You Go

The day before you go:

- Check in online
- Double-check that you have important documents
- Guidebooks
- Double-check seats and flight times
- Get money from the bank and notify credit card companies

Checking in online

This is simple and can save a lot of time at the airport. You can do it whether you are checking bags or carrying them on. Simply go to the website of the airline—they will have a page for online check-in. You'll need to know your confirmation number and how many bags you are checking. You print your boarding pass at home or have it sent to your phone and off you go.

By printing your boarding pass at home or having it sent to your phone, you can go straight to the gate if you have no bags to check. If you are checking bags, when you arrive at the airport bring the document to the airline's online check-in kiosk. This line is usually much shorter than the line at the desk. You will enter your confirmation number on the kiosk's touch screen, the agent will take your bags and ticket them, and you will print your boarding pass at the airport. This is a must, if at all possible. Now, if you are someplace where you cannot do this or you are departing from a tiny airport, it is probably not as necessary. However, O'Hare is our home airport and with the long lines of travelers there waiting to pick up their tickets and boarding passes, printing ahead of time is a necessity. If you are someplace without a computer or printer, get the app that allows you to retrieve the boarding information on your phone.

As for luggage, the lighter, the better. If your child's bag is too heavy, you will end up carrying it in addition to your own. Also, consider what the children will need when you get to your destination. If they will need lots of toys when they get there, stick some in the suitcase. If your destination will be entertaining enough, then go light on the American Girl dolls, Legos, and other large items.

I used to be hardcore on the electronic games and would make my kids read and play card games. I have eased up on that in recent years, and now they travel with iPods and other electronics. I still wish they would play cards and color or something. You will have to decide what you want them to do. This also depends on the ages of the children and the length of the flight. The longer the flight, the more you need to keep them entertained.

Important documents

- Passports or ID
- Health insurance cards
- Flight confirmations
- Hotel confirmations
- Tickets for anything
- Activity reservations

Guidebooks

It is nice to have a few guidebooks to consult so you can change plans or add an activity if needed. I have also changed hotels when I got someplace and didn't like it. I was able to look up an alternative and find the phone number to make a new reservation. You can pack guidebooks in your suitcase if they are heavy.

Double-check seats and flight times

It is always a good idea to double-check your seat assignments and departure times so that you do not miss your flight. I always recommend checking your seats so that you are not spread out all over the plane and trying to move people to accommodate your family. You also might be able to get more legroom. You should be able to find out how much extra that will cost you.

Get money from the bank and notify credit card companies that you will be traveling

I recommend traveling with $300 or so, but you will have to determine what you are comfortable with. Some people travel with mostly cash and others with very little. You just don't want to get someplace and have no money. I would err on the side of caution and bring more money. Also, let your credit card companies know you will be traveling so that if you make purchases far from home they don't cut you off as a safety precaution. If you live in Chicago and all of a sudden start making purchases in Florida they might become suspicious.

The Day of Travel

The day of travel:

- Wear comfortable clothes
- Make sure you have all the tickets, passports, driver's licenses, and other paperwork
- Bring a coat, if necessary
- Don't forget anyone's suitcase
- Leave lots of extra time
- Determine seating arrangement on plane
- Give the kids money or budget for trip

You'll have to take off your shoes, jackets, jewelry, and belts at the security checkpoint, so wear comfortable clothes without much that will need to be removed. I also recommend shoes that are easy to slip on and off. Wear socks so you don't have to go barefoot on the airport floor.

What to wear on the day of travel:

- Comfortable clothes
- Socks (unless you don't mind going barefoot through security)
- No jewelry, belts, or other items that will need to be removed for security
- Shoes that are easy to remove
- Coat, if required

Have a folder for all travel documents, including:

- Tickets
- Reservations
- Rental car confirmation
- Locations of restaurants
- Itinerary

Bring passports and driver's licenses for all travelers over seventeen and those who look over seventeen. Sometimes the TSA agent cannot tell the kid's ages and it is better to be prepared with at least a school ID.

Count the suitcases and make sure everyone's is accounted for before departure.

Leave yourself extra time.

Traveling with kids is a slow process. It takes time to get through security, go to the bathroom, get to the gate, etc. My kids love to eat at the airport and shop for magazines and so on. Leave yourself two hours prior to departure time.

Seating

The seating arrangement is always an issue. You can put the kids together if they are old enough. Otherwise, Mom can sit with some of the kids and Dad with the others. Figure this out prior to getting on the plane.

Budget

Give the kids a spending-money budget on the trip. This prevents them from begging for something in every shop.

During or After Your Trip

Blog with www.mytripjournal.com, www.wordpress.com, or www. blogger.com. You can create a travel journal with pictures and comments.

At www.IgoUgo.com, you can post journals and photos online.

Flickr.com, Shutterfly.com, and Snapfish.com are great for down-loading photos.

So once you have taken all those great photos, what do you do? Here are a few ideas:

Make a postcard at www.postagram.com.

Make a photo album on Apple, Shutterfly, or any other photo website.

Make an iPhoto journal with the iPhoto app.

Put together a slide show; iPhoto is the easiest application for this.

Make an iPhone case at www.casetagram.com.

Make coasters at www.imagesnap.com.

Part V
Travel Tips

Travel Tips

- Lock up passports and valuables when traveling internationally.
- If your passport is stolen, go to www.travel.state.gov.
- Beware of pickpockets.
- Keep recent photos of children in your wallet, in case the kids get lost.
- Don't look like a tourist by carrying lots of cash and maps.
- Allow enough time at the airport and eat before the flight. Children are not good on planes when they are hungry.
- Fly early in the day. Flying during nap time or at night only means fussy kids.
- Travel at nonpeak times when your chances are better for an extra seat.
- Have the kids run around before the trip to use up some energy.
- Use the restroom before getting on the plane or in the car.
- Have the hotel concierge arrange excursions for you.
- Buy museum passes online to avoid long lines.

Tips for Saving Money

International:

- Switch your cell phone to airplane mode to stop roaming. This way you won't get a huge bill for roaming charges when you return home.
- Use your debit card to get cash and your credit card to make purchases.
- Check www.kayak.com and www.vayama.com for the best prices on international flights.
- Check these websites for cheap fares: www.mobissimo.com, www.dohop.com, www.bing.com, and www.vayama.com.
- Make a copy of your passport and credit cards in case anything gets lost.
- Only bring a few credit cards. You will not need all the department store cards.
- Let the credit card companies know you will be traveling overseas so that they don't cut you off for unusual activity on your card.
- Change a little money when you get to the airport, but not too much. The exchange rate at airports will not be very good. ATMs give the best exchange rate.
- Use your debit card to get cash and you'll get a good rate with low to no extra charges. Banks are fine too, although they are often closed when you need them. In many countries, banks close for several hours at lunch and often have bank holidays, so it's easiest just to plan on using ATMs.

Domestic:

- Vacation packages can save you some money, but make sure you know what you are getting. The quality of hotels is sometimes unknown and the flight times are often off-peak. However, if you are interested in vacation packages check out:

- Expedia.com
- Hotwire.com
- Orbitz.com
- Travelocity.com
- American and United Airlines – www.aa.com and www. United.com
- Travel agents

- Fly on Tuesday or Wednesday since these are less popular and therefore cheaper
- Check Expedia's Trend Tracker; it gives you the least expensive time to visit a place. It is easiest to just search "Expedia Trend Tracker".
- For fare predictions, check Farecast.com and Yapta.com.
- CheapOair.com also provides really good fares, but watch the connections—sometimes they are kind of unusual.
- For discount theater tickets, check out BroadwayBox.com and Goldstar.com.
- For discount lodging, visit LastMinuteTravel.com.

International Travel Health Tips

When you are going to places with less than optimal sanitation, you simply cannot drink the water. You must drink only bottled water, and that means when brushing your teeth as well.

Do not eat any unpeeled fruits or vegetables in countries with lower sanitation standards. I tell my kids that it is their time off from any fruits or vegetables—I would rather not risk it.

Use hand sanitizer and give everyone a Pepto-Bismol tablet every day, just to ward off any possibility of getting sick.

You could try the anti-jet lag diet. You can look this up online for the details, but you start four days before you leave. Avoid alcohol and caffeine. Start with a high protein breakfast and lunch and a high carbohydrate dinner. On day two, you eat just light salads and soups. Day three is the same as the first day, and day four is the same as day two. When you arrive, you eat a high protein breakfast. It is supposed to help with jet lag. I have tried it with minimal results. There are also medications you can take. I also just allow everyone a little nap of a couple of hours when we arrive and that seems to really help.

Travel Insurance

When it comes to travel insurance, there are three types:

- Trip cancellation
- Emergency medical
- Medical evacuation

Trip cancellation covers, obviously, trip cancellation, but also lost bags and any emergency medical treatment that may be required. This is purchased when you make your flight or travel arrangements.

Emergency medical insurance can be obtained through your health insurance company.

Medical evacuation insurance can be purchased by one of the following companies:

- MedjetAssist.com
- TravelGuard.com
- TravelexInsurance.com
- IMGlobal.com
- CSAtravelpro.com
- Allianztravelinsurance.com
- www.insuremytrip.com

If you are traveling to a remote country with hospitals that would not be up to your standards, be sure to get the medical evacuation insurance.

Miscellaneous Tips:

- Keep phone numbers in a safe place.
- Bring converters for electronics and adaptors to fit the plug configuration at your destination.
- Call your cell phone company to sign up for the international plan for your destination. If you don't, you either won't get service or you will have a huge bill when you get home. You might also buy an Internet phone, a cell phone when you arrive, or use Skype. Turn off your phone's roaming feature to prevent huge charges on e-mails and texting as well.

Part VI

Websites, Apps, and Blogs

Websites, Apps and Blogs

There are hundreds of apps for travel. You can get an app for almost anything, from exchanging currency and finding a flight, hotel, or restaurant to packing, communicating, and photo journaling. Here are a few recommended apps.

Websites:

Flights

Kayak.com—searches for flights, compares fares on a variety of airlines
Expedia.com and Orbitz.com—search for flights, hotels, rental cars, etc.
United.com—United Airlines
AA.com—American Airlines
Southwest.com—Southwest Airlines
Delta.com—Delta Airlines
CheapOair.com—offers flights at cheap prices, but sometimes you have odd connections, change airports for your connection, or do not know what airline you will be flying until close to the departure date
Dealbase.com—compares price on hotels and flights, compares Expedia, Priceline, Hotels.com, and Kayak
SeatExpert.com and SeatGuru.com—give you best seats available
TripIt.com—organizes airline tickets, hotel bookings, and other reservations
MileWise.com—helps you decide whether to purchase tickets with frequent flyer miles or cash
WebJet.com—flight comparisons
Vayama.com—cheap European plane tickets

Skypicker.com—European plane tickets

Accommodations

Tripadvisor.com – offers vacation rentals, hotels, flights, and restaurants
Cfares.com and itasoftware.com—compare fares, but are not booking sites
TripKick.com—helps you select best rooms and hotels for select cities; not a booking site
Hotels.com—offers hotels around the world at good prices
Venere.com—search site with more European options, 100,000 hotels, B&Bs, and apartments
PAP.fr—finds apartments for rent in France (site hard to navigate unless you speak French)
HomeAway.com—finds vacation rentals
WorldwideToursDirectory.com—lists many of the tour operators around the world

Simplifying

BabiesTravelLite.com—delivers all the stuff for your little one so it is there when you arrive (food, diapers, toys, books, medicine, travel gear, etc.)
Flyingwithkids.com—travel tips and links
Whatsonwhen.com—lists events, from art festivals to sporting events and beyond, in your selected city on your selected dates
Flickr.com—photo sharing site
Audible.com—books read aloud downloadable to iPhone, etc.
Opentable.com—makes a dinner reservation in many cities online
DishTip.com—restaurant suggestions
MenuPages.com—menus of nearby restaurants
VirtualTourist.com—Forum with reviews of popular destinations and sites

Budget

RedWeek.com—list of timeshares to sell
AAA.com—travel discounts
Craigslist and EBay—theme park discounts
LastMinuteTravel.com – Deals on flights, hotels, cars, etc.
BroadwayBox.com—discount theater tickets

Apps:

I would search for these in your phone's app store. Some have websites too.

Flights

OntheFlyTravel—compares flight prices, no booking
Flight Board—lists flight arrival and departure information at airports around the world
Next Flight—if you miss your flight, finds the next one for you
Momondo—finds flights in Europe
SeatGuru—finds the best airplane seats available
Skyscanner—flight search engine; if you are flexible on dates and where to go, helps you find best fares
Bing Travel—predicts whether the price of a ticket will go up or down

Cruises

Cruise Finder and CruiseWise—search for best prices on cruises
   Packing – *The following are helpful when it comes to packing*
   PackTMPack & Go
   Packing List
   Packing Pal
   TripList
   Packing Panic!
   uPackingList
   GetPacked
   Packing Pro

Communications

Help Call—emergency numbers anywhere in the world
Skype—allows you to call home for free
Truphone—app that turns an iPhone into an Internet phone

Entertainment

Road Trip Fun—games to play on a road trip
State Plate Hunt—checklist of states
Road Trip Bingo—bingo card for iPhone; search for items found on a road trip
Cool Mad Libs—app version of Mad Libs game
Would You Prefer?—app version of Would You Rather? game
SpinArt—remember spin art from when you were a kid?
Urbanspoon—lists best local restaurants

Educational

HearPlanet—tells about sites anywhere in the world
World Customs & Cultures—tells of customs anywhere in the world
Weather Channel—weather app
Babelingo—language translator
WHERE—local information, including restaurants, things to do, sites to see, etc.
Travel Pro—currency converter, language translator, packing assistant, airfare and cruise pro
Frommer's Travel Tools—tip calculator, packing list, currency converter, city guides, trivia
Perfect World Clock—checks time anywhere in the world
BackCountry Navigator PRO GPS—uses GPS maps to find terrain suiting any camper's needs
WeatherBugElite—keeps an eye on the weather for any neighborhood
Wikitude—direct your phone toward point of interest and information about it will appear on screen

Photography

Trip Journal—creates a virtual journal with your notes, photos, and maps

Pano—allows you to make a panoramic shot by combining a series of photos

Instagram—Combines picture-taking software with social networking

Blogs:

Travelingwithkids.com

Traveling-kids.blogspot.com

CiaoBambino.com

TravelSavvyMom.com

WeJustGotBack.com

DeliciousBaby.com

HaveBabyWillTravel.com

BackpacktoBuggy.com

HipTravelMama.com

WanderMom.com

MotherofAllTrips.com

AdventuresforFamilies.net

BabyLovestoTravel.com

TravelswithBaby.com

TravelingMamas.com

Travels with Children, www.minnemom.com

What a Trip, www.nancydbrown.com

Part VII

Fun Vacation Ideas

Best Family Resorts

- Kaanapali Beach Hotel, Maui, Hawaii
- The Greenbrier, White Sulphur Springs, West Virginia
- Little Dix Bay, Virgin Gorda, British Virgin Islands
- Ritz-Carlton, Cancun, Mexico
- Disney's Pop Century Resort, Lake Buena Vista, Florida
- Four Seasons Resort Costa Rica at Peninsula Papagayo, Costa Rica
- Fairmont Kea Lani, Maui, Hawaii
- Breakers Hotel in Palm Beach, Florida
- Winnetu Oceanside Resort, Martha's Vineyard, Massachusetts
- Kingsmill Resort & Spa, Williamsburg, Virginia
- Loews Coronado Bay Resort & Spa, San Diego, California
- Colony Beach & Tennis Resort, Longboat Key, Florida
- Ritz-Carlton, Amelia Island, Florida
- Tyler Place Family Resort, Highgate Springs, Vermont
- Ojai Valley Inn & Spa, Ojai, California
- Four Seasons Lana'i at Manele Bay, Lanai City, Hawaii
- Club Med Sandpiper, Port Saint Lucie, Florida

Sources: Travel & Leisure, parents.com

Best Beaches

- Maui, Hawaii
- US Virgin Islands
- Hawaii (the Big Island)
- Honolulu, Oahu, Hawaii
- Outer Banks, North Carolina
- Miami Beach, Florida
- San Diego, California
- Fort Lauderdale, Florida
- Myrtle Beach, South Carolina
- Los Angeles, California
- Bondi Beach, Australia
- Catalina Island, California
- Fiji Islands
- Corfu, Greece
- Petit Saint Vincent, Grenadines
- Kauai, Hawaii
- Canary Islands, Spain
- Maldives
- Playa del Carmen, Mexico
- South Beach, Miami, Florida
- Main Beach, East Hampton, New York
- Seychelles
- Phi Phi Island, Thailand

Source: www.Forbes.com,.travel.usnews.com/

Top 25 Tennis Resorts

- Kiawah Island Golf Resort, South Carolina
- Ranch Valencia, California
- La Quinta Resort & Club, California
- Bio-Hotel Stanglwirt, Tirol, Austria
- Wild Dunes, South Carolina
- Caneel Bay, US Virgin Islands
- Mauna Kea Beach Hotel, Hawaii
- Palmetto Dunes Oceanfront Resort, South Carolina
- Top Notch Resort & Spa, Vermont
- Longboat Key Club & Resort, Florida
- JW Marriott Desert Springs Resort & Spa, California
- TOPS'L Beach & Racquet Resort, Florida
- Four Seasons Resort, Nevis
- Sea Pines Resort, South Carolina
- Broadmoor, Colorado
- Ponte Vedra Inn & Club, Florida
- The Boulders, Arizona
- Boca Raton Resort & Club, Florida
- Sandestin Golf & Beach Resort, Florida
- Wintergreen Resort, Virginia
- Punta Mita Resort, Nayarit, Mexico
- Four Seasons Resort, Texas
- Waterville Valley Resort, New Hampshire
- Saddlebrook Resort, Florida
- Naples Grande Beach Resort, Florida

Source: www.tennisresortsonline.com

Top 25 Golf Resorts

Bandon Dunes, Oregon
Inn at Spanish Bay, Pebble Beach, California
American Club, Wisconsin
Cloister & Lodge at Sea Island, Georgia
Greenbrier, West Virginia
Four Seasons Hualalai, Ka'upulehu, Hawaii
Ritz-Carlton, Kapalua, Hawaii
One & Only Ocean Club Atlantis, Paradise Island, Bahamas
Four Seasons Punta Mita, Nayarit, Mexico
Sand Lane, Barbados
Broadmoor, Colorado
One & Only Palmilla, Los Cabos, Mexico
Pinehurst, North Carolina
Four Seasons Lana'i, Hawaii
Inn at Palmetto Bluff, South Carolina
Fox Harb'r Golf Resort, Nova Scotia
Kiawah Island, South Carolina
Ritz-Carlton Bachelor Gulch, Colorado
St. Regis Princeville, Hawaii
Wynn Las Vegas, Nevada
Ritz-Carlton Dove Mountain, Arizona
Ritz-Carlton Lodge at Reynolds Plantation, Georgia
Fairmont Banff, Alberta, Canada
Four Seasons Resort, Scottsdale, Arizona

Source: www.golfdigest.com

Top 10 National Parks

Death Valley, CA
Yellowstone, WY
Bryce, UT
Volcanoes, HI
Grand Canyon, AZ
Yosemite, CA
Crater Lake, OR
Arches, UT
Everglades, FL
Acadia, ME

Source: www.abcnews.go.com

Best European Vacations

- Barcelona
- Paris
- Lisbon
- Berlin
- Budapest
- Prague
- Amsterdam
- London
- Istanbul
- Madrid
- Rome
- Florence
- Copenhagen
- Crete
- Zurich
- St. Petersburg
- Edinburgh
- Mykonos
- Krakow
- Glasgow

Source: U.S. News

Best Family Cruise Lines

- Royal Caribbean
- Carnival
- NCL
- Disney
- Princess

Source: www.cruisecritic.com

Best US Ski Resorts

Deer Valley, Utah
Vail, Colorado
Whistler Blackcomb, Canada
Snowmass, Colorado
Sun Valley, Idaho
Park City, Utah
Beaver Creek, Colorado
Steamboat, Colorado
Breckenridge, Colorado
Telluride, Colorado

Source: www.skimag.com

Best Ski Resorts in Europe

Andorra
Pal Arinsal
Soldeu
Pas de la Casa

Austria
Ischgl
Kitzbuhel
Saint Anton am Arlberg
Zell am See

Bulgaria
Bansko
Borovets
Pamporovo

France
Chamonix and Argentiere
Courchevel
Brides-les-Bains
La Grave & Les Deux Alpes
La Tania
Les Arcs & La Plagne
Meribel
Val d'Isere & Tignes
Val Thorens

Germany
Garmisch-Partenkirchen

Italy
Cortina d'Ampezzo
Selva di Val Gardena

Norway
Narvik

Sweden
Are
Riksgransen

Switzerland
Zermatt
Verbier
Saint Moritz
Davos Klosters

Source: www.thebestskiresorts.info/

Best Ski Resorts Outside of Europe and North America

Argentina
Las Lenas
San Carlos de Bariloche

Australia
Thredbo
Perisher Blue
Jindabyne

Chile
Portillo
Valle Nevado, La Parva, and El Colorado

India
Gulmarg
Manali

Japan
Happo-One and Shiga Kogen

New Zealand
Aoraki/Mount Cook
Mount Ruapehu
Treble Cone

Source: www.thebestskiresorts.info

Best Skateboard Parks

Black Pearl Skate Park, Cayman Islands
Woodward West Camp, Stallion Springs, California
Encitas YMCA, Encitas, California
Battle Ground Skatepark, Battle Ground, Washington
Playstation Skatepark, London
Millenium Skatepark, Calgary
Trinidad Skatepark, Trinidad, Colorado
Louisville Extreme Park, Louisville, Kentucky

Source: www.americansbestonlline.com/

10 Best Amusement Parks in America

Cedar Point, Sandusky, Ohio
Disney World, Orlando, Florida
King's Island, Mason, Ohio
Schlitterbahn, New Braunfels, Texas
Disneyland, Anaheim, California
Busch Gardens, Williamsburg, Virginia
Universal Studios, Orlando, Florida
Knoebels Amusement Park, Elysburg, Pennsylvania
Six Flags, Gurnee, Illinois
Legoland, Carlsbad, California

Source: www.wrsol.com

America's 7 Best Ballparks

- Oriole Park at Camden Yards. Baltimore, Maryland
- Safeco Field. Seattle, Washington
- Citi Field, New York (and honorable mention to Yankee Stadium, New York)
- Wrigley Field, Chicago
- AT&T Park, San Francisco
- Fenway Park, Boston
- PNC Park, Pittsburgh

Source: Abcnews.go.com

Appedices

Appendix A
Getting Started Worksheet

Purpose of this vacation:

_____

_____

_____

_____

Ages of children:

_____

_____

_____

_____

Family interests:

_____

_____

_____

_____

Family temperament:

_____

_____

_____

How much hassle we can tolerate:

_____

_____

_____

_____

Budget:

_____

_____

_____

_____

Ideas to consider:

_____

_____

_____

_____

Babysitting needs:

_____

_____

_____

_____

Appendix B
Budget Calculator

	Option A	Option B
Airfare	$	
Accommodations	$	
Rental car/taxis	$	
Meals	$	
Activities	$	
Child care	$	
Purchases	$	
Subtotal	$	
Unexpected costs (10%)	$	
Total	$	

Appendix C
Vacation Planning Checklists

Six months or more in advance:

- ❏ Book plane tickets
- ❏ Reserve hotel or condo

One month in advance:

- ❏ Reserve rental car
- ❏ Schedule any activities
- ❏ Make dinner reservations
- ❏ Schedule golf tee times, tennis court reservations, spa appointments, ski school or instructors

One week in advance:

- ❏ Pack
- ❏ Confirm flight times have not changed
- ❏ Order transportation to and from airport
- ❏ Send anything you will need (golf clubs, skis, etc.)
- ❏ Order diapers, groceries, etc. to be delivered at destination
- ❏ Confirm that your plane seats are in desired configuration
- ❏ Buy anything you will need for trip, including special clothes, toiletries, games

The day before departure:

- ❏ Check in online
- ❏ Pack carry-on
- ❏ Pack all paperwork
- ❏ Bring guidebooks
- ❏ Go to the bank

- ❏ Call credit card companies to let them know you will be traveling

The day of travel:

- ❏ Wear comfortable clothes
- ❏ Make sure you have all tickets, passports, driver's licenses, and other paperwork
- ❏ Bring a coat, if necessary
- ❏ Don't forget anyone's suitcase
- ❏ Leave lots of extra time
- ❏ Determine seating arrangement on plane
- ❏ Give kids money or budget for trip

Plane Ticket Checklist:

If you do not need to be loyal to one airline:

- ❏ Check price on Kayak, which will compare Expedia, Priceline, Hotwire, Orbitz, and CheapOair
- ❏ Check price on airline's website
- ❏ Check Southwest Airlines
- ❏ Consider schedule as well as price
- ❏ Reserve seats, if possible
- ❏ Use miles, if applicable

Accommodation Checklist:

- ❏ Book condo or hotel
- ❏ Check out reviews on TripAdvisor, Yelp, and other critiques
- ❏ Read guidebook suggestions
- ❏ Talk to friends for recommendations
- ❏ Read travel magazines for suggestions

International Travel Checklist:

Book Plane Tickets

- ❏ www.opodo.co.uk
- ❏ www.openjet.com
- ❏ www.applefares.com
- ❏ www.skyscanner.net
- ❏ www.whichbudget.com

Book Accommodations

- ❏ www.windowsonitaly.com
- ❏ www.rentalo.com
- ❏ www.vrbo.com

Take Care of Paperwork and Shots

- ❏ Check the CDC website for required shots at www.cdc.gov.
- ❏ Make sure passports are current. Passports are required for everyone, even if your baby is a week old. Information can be accessed at www.travel.state.gov/passport.
- ❏ Check your destination country's website for visa requirements or www.travel.state.gov/visa.

Rental Car Checklist:

- ❏ Reserve rental car.
- ❏ Sign up for preferred rental program to save time at check-in.
- ❏ Determine what size car you'll need.

- ❏ Determine whether you'll need an automatic or manual (stick shift).
- ❏ Determine whether you will purchase prepaid gas.
- ❏ Determine if you'll need extras, such as GPS, baby seat, or ski rack.
- ❏ Determine whether you'll need to purchase insurance from the rental car company or if you'll have coverage through your own auto insurance.

Activities Checklist:

- ❏ Check guidebooks—Fodor's, Frommer's, Blue Planet, and any others.
- ❏ Google "top ten things to do with kids in____(destination)."
- ❏ Check with the hotel concierge for recommendations.
- ❏ Ask friends for recommendations.
- ❏ Mix kids' activities with culture to make sure there is something for everyone.
- ❏ Consider what your family likes to do.
- ❏ Ask the kids what they want to do.
- ❏ Come up with a tentative plan.
- ❏ Make reservations for activities, dinner, and golf, tennis, skiing, spa or anything else you might need.

What to wear on the day of travel:

- ❏ Comfortable clothes
- ❏ Socks (unless you don't mind going barefoot through security)
- ❏ No jewelry, belts, or other items that will need to be removed for security
- ❏ Shoes that are easy to remove
- ❏ Coat, if required

Have a folder for all travel documents, including:

- ❏ Tickets
- ❏ Reservations
- ❏ Rental car confirmation
- ❏ Locations of restaurants
- ❏ Itinerary

Miscellaneous Tips Checklist:

- ❏ Make copies of credit cards and passports.
- ❏ Keep phone numbers in a safe place.
- ❏ Bring converters for electronics and adaptors to fit the plug configuration at your destination.
- ❏ Call your cell phone company to sign up for the international plan for your destination. If you don't, you either won't get service or you will have a huge bill when you get home. You might also buy an Internet phone, a cell phone when you arrive, or use Skype. Turn off your phone's roaming feature to prevent huge charges on e-mails and texting as well.

Appendix D
Packing List

Mom's Bag:

- Books (paperback only), magazines, and newspapers (don't make it too heavy)
- Prescription medications
- iPod and iPad, plus earphones
- Card games
- Glasses and sunglasses
- Jewelry
- Necessary electronics (the lighter, the better)

Snacks (make sure you have enough to keep everyone full for the duration of the flight plus extra for delays)

- Gum, lollipop, or sippy cup for earaches on airplane descent
- All creams and gels must fit into a small baggie and cannot be larger than three ounces
- Hand sanitizer
- Bottles, food, snacks (check airplane rules regarding liquids and foods)
- Diapers and wipes
- Change of clothes (maybe for you too, in case you get barfed on)
- Dramamine or other medicine for car/motion sickness
- Toys, books, games

Kids' Bags:

- Headphones for movies

- Toys
- Coloring books
- Card games
- Electronic games
- Disposable camera (so they can take their own pictures)
- Journal (to write down their memories)
- Paperback books
- Mad Libs
- Jump rope
- Snacks
- Movie from Redbox if there is on at your local grocery and if you are going somewhere with a DVD player

In the Suitcase:

- First aid kit (bring kids' medicine; it is hard to find at airports and small groceries)
- Tylenol
- Decongestant
- Cough medicine
- Allergy medicine
- Band-Aids
- Solarcaine (for sunburns)_
- Suntan lotion
- Pepto-Bismol
- Bug spray
- Hand sanitizer
- Vitamins
- Dramamine and wrist bands for motion sickness

Toiletries bag (or use what is at the hotel)

- Shampoo
- Conditioner
- Comb or brush

- Body lotion
- Bath gel
- Toothbrush and toothpaste
- Contact lenses and cleanser, saline, etc.
- Deodorant
- Razor
- Makeup
- Jewelry
- Feminine hygiene products
- Facial products (wash, moisturizer, blemish cream, etc.)
- Shower cap and hair ties
- Tweezers and small scissors

Clothes

It depends where you are going, but you might need:

- Diapers (two-day supply and buy the rest at your destination; they are bulky)
- Socks, stockings
- Underwear
- Pajamas
- Swimsuits and cover-ups
- T-shirts
- Dress shirts
- Collared shirts
- Shorts
- Casual pants
- Dress pants
- Skirts with tops
- Dresses
- Sweaters
- Blazers and ties
- Belt
- Outerwear
- Umbrella

- Workout clothes
- Golf clothes
- Tennis clothes
- Ski clothes
- Pillowcase for dirty clothes

- Shoes
- Sandals
- Beach
- Gym
- Tennis
- Fancy
- Loafers

- Electronics
- Phone
- iPad
- Camera
- Chargers
- Earphones
- Laptop computer

Important Documents:

- Passports or ID
- Health insurance cards
- Flight confirmations
- Hotel confirmations
- Tickets for anything

Bibliography

Books:

      Stellin, Susan. *How to Travel Practically Anywhere*. New York: Houghton Mifflin, 2006.

Willdorf, Nina. *The Smart Family's Passport*. Philadelphia: Quirk Books, 2010.

Magazines:

      National Geographic Traveler

      Travel + Leisure

      Town & Country

      Conde Nast Traveler

Websites:

      www.ricksteves.com

      www.babble.com

      www.alltraveltips.com

      www.lifehacker.com

AT&T Insider, www.insider/att.com

Acknowledgments

I would like to thank my parents for teaching me the love of travel. Without their inspiration I would never have visited so many wonderful places. I would also like to thank my in-laws for taking us year after year to Switzerland. Most importantly, I would like to thank my husband, who accompanied me on our quest to show our kids the world. Finally, I would like to thank my editor, Eric Ziegenhagen, who helped me organize and consolidate all my thoughts and words.

Made in the USA
Charleston, SC
15 December 2013